Cambridge E

C000046966

Elements in Politics and :

edited by
Erin Aeran Chung
The Johns Hopkins University
Mary Alice Haddad
Wesleyan University, Connecticut
Benjamin L. Read
University of California, Santa Cruz

THE DIGITAL TRANSFORMATION AND JAPAN'S POLITICAL ECONOMY

Ulrike Schaede
University of California San Diego
Kay Shimizu
University of Pittsburgh

CAMBRIDGE
UNIVERSITY PRESS

CAMBRIDGE
UNIVERSITY PRESS

University Printing House, Cambridge CB2 8BS, United Kingdom

One Liberty Plaza, 20th Floor, New York, NY 10006, USA

477 Williamstown Road, Port Melbourne, VIC 3207, Australia

314–321, 3rd Floor, Plot 3, Splendor Forum, Jasola District Centre,
New Delhi – 110025, India

103 Penang Road, #05–06/07, Visioncrest Commercial, Singapore 238467

Cambridge University Press is part of the University of Cambridge.

It furthers the University's mission by disseminating knowledge in the pursuit of
education, learning, and research at the highest international levels of excellence.

www.cambridge.org
Information on this title: www.cambridge.org/9781108925709
DOI: 10.1017/9781108921015

© Ulrike Schaede, and Kay Shimizu 2022

First published 2022

A catalogue record for this publication is available from the British Library.

ISBN 978-1-108-92570-9 Paperback
ISSN 2632-7368 (online)
ISSN 2632-735X (print)

Cambridge University Press has no responsibility for the persistence or accuracy of
URLs for external or third-party internet websites referred to in this publication
and does not guarantee that any content on such websites is, or will remain,
accurate or appropriate.

The Digital Transformation And Japan's Political Economy

Elements in Politics and Society in East Asia

DOI: 10.1017/9781108921015
First published online: May 2022

Ulrike Schaede
University of California San Diego

Kay Shimizu
University of Pittsburgh

Author for correspondence: Ulrike Schaede, uschaede@ucsd.edu

Abstract: The digital transformation and demographic change are usually seen as two separate but equally threatening events that foreshadow job replacement, industrial decline, and social bifurcation. Because Japan is the world's frontrunner in demographic change with an ageing and shrinking society, it is facing these two disruptions at the exact same time. This creates a "lucky moment," as it presents an opportunity to employ one as a solution for the problems caused by the other. For example, Japan's traditional sectors are replaced by digital systems that demand fewer people while offering new jobs. Emerging technologies are opening fresh opportunities for Japanese companies to compete globally. The twin disruptions are also upending Japan's political economy. As companies reinvent business strategies and employees reskill to pursue individual careers, the state is reorganizing to find a new role in balancing the unfolding demands of the digital economy.

Keywords: Digital transformation, demographic change, deep technology, agrotech, AI, industrial policy, ageing society, labor shortage, reskilling

ISBNs: 9781108925709 (PB), 9781108921015 (OC)
ISSNs: 2632-7368 (online), 2632-735X (print)

Contents

1 Introduction   1

2 Definitions: The Digital Transformation (DX)
   and Demographic Change   6

3 Context: Japan's Political Economy in the Post-WWII Era   19

4 The DX and Business: New Technologies, Industries,
   and Global Strategies   32

5 The DX and People: New Employment Patterns and
   Reskilling   46

6 The DX and the State: Toward a New Political Economy   57

7 Conclusion: The DX and Japan's New Political Economy   66

   References   70

1 Introduction

Most analyses of Japan since the beginning of the twenty-first century portray a scenario of doom and gloom. As the world prepares for the digital transformation (DX), it is often assumed that leadership in future industries such as big data analysis, the cloud, and artificial intelligence will belong to the United States and China.[1] Japanese companies are generally seen as too slow or too weak to compete, and Japan's economic structures are considered too ossified, stagnant, and unproductive.[2] What is more, Japan is the first country in the world to face rapid demographic change, with the population predicted to shrink by 25 percent in the next three decades, from 126 million to fewer than 100 million people by 2050. By 2040, 36 percent of Japan's population will be older than sixty-five years (Cabinet Office 2020a). This has not only made labor shortage a certainty but has also raised grave concerns about the future fabric of Japanese society and economy, as well as its sustainable prosperity and social security.

To many observers, these two trends' co-occurrence means Japan is destined for obsolescence. However, if one looks beyond the macroeconomic indicators and demographic prognostications, the story is not so simple. Together, the digital transformation and demographic change create a window of opportunity for Japan, where the changing needs of labor are creating space for companies to explore and shift to new strategies, which in turn are facilitating a rewriting of the mutual rights and obligations between government, business, and labor that defined Japan's twentieth-century political economy.

The term "digital transformation" refers to the great advances in computing powers and analytical techniques, as well as communication and vision/sensing technologies that combine to create a new world of 5G-enabled constant connectivity, autonomous systems and robotics, blockchain, artificial intelligence and machine learning (AI/ML), data mining, and governance through "the cloud." For industry, these advances coalesce into what has been termed "industry 4.0," that is, the arrival of digital manufacturing, which will upend what we know about operations management. For humans, they bring the next step of our evolution, into "society 5.0," namely, a constantly connected society based on autonomous systems for most service needs.[3] The digital transformation will be borderless,

---

[1] For example, "Why China can race ahead in digital economy," *CGTN*, September 18, 2019.

[2] For example, Glosserman (2019), McKinsey and ACCJ (2021), and "Too rich, too comfortable: Why Japan is so resistant to change even as disaster looms," *Quartz*, April 2, 2019.

[3] The term "industry 4.0," also called the "fourth industrial revolution," was coined in the early 2010s by German trade associations lobbying for government investments in future technologies. It soon became a rallying cry for increasing competitiveness in Japan, which added the concept of "society 5.0" to refer to the next step in human evolution, following the stages of hunting/gathering and the agricultural, industrial, and information societies; www8.cao.go.jp/cstp/eng lish/society5_0/index.html

ubiquitous, and inescapable, and it has already begun. It is about to affect all industries, societies, and continents in similar ways. The nature of competition, the meaning of production, the demarcation of industrial sectors, and the identity and assignments of workers will all evolve. In many countries, the realization of these impending changes has brought fears of a world taken over by robots, riddled by social displacement and distress, governed by algorithms, and regulated in ways that favor machines over humans (e.g., Brynjolfsson and McAfee 2016; Ford 2016; Acemoglu and Restrepo 2020).

Japan is certainly not the only country to face the digital disruption, nor is it the only country facing demographic change. But what is special about Japan's situation is the timing: Because Japan's society is ageing and shrinking earlier and faster than any other advanced nation, the demographic shock and the digital transformation are arriving at exactly the same time. To visualize this coincidence, Figure 1 shows Japan's working population in the top solid line (see Section 2 for comparative demographics), as well as

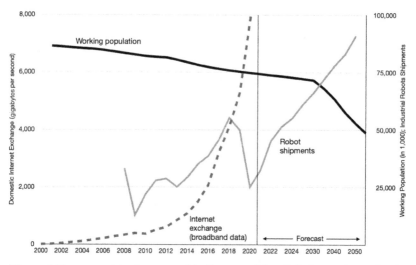

Figure 1 Demographic change and indicators of the digital transformation in Japan

Note: Decline in working population (in 1,000 people, right axis, top line), industrial robot shipments (right axis), and broadband-based data use, peak traffic in December of each year, left axis[4]

---

[4]　Constructed from: Population: NIPSSR, Population Projections for Japan, 2001–2050, www.ipss.go
.jp/pp-newest/e/ppfj02/ppfj02.pdf; Robots: IFR 2020 World Robotics Report, https://ifr.org/ifr-press-
releases/news/record-2.7-million-robots-work-in-factories-around-the-globe; Japan broadband data
use: Ministry of Communication, www.soumu.go.jp/menu_news/s-news/01kiban04_02000160.html

two indicators of technological change. The first is the rapid increase in fixed-line broadband data exchange (dashed line). This began to rise in the 2010s and increased exponentially with the 2019–20 COVID-19 pandemic and the shift to telework. The gray line represents a second indicator, the number of shipments of multiuse industrial robots. While it declined during COVID-19, it is now conservatively estimated to grow at least at 5 percent year-over-year.

This coincidence presents a window of opportunity, a "lucky moment," for Japan. The simultaneous arrival of the two disruptions – ageing society and shrinking workforce *cum* digitization of industry and society – brings not so much a threat, but rather, the solution. Far from throwing Japan into obsolescence, they offer an opportunity to combine two negatives into one positive. Japan may emerge a stronger economy and society for it, as each disruption can solve the problems caused by the other. The arrival of automated systems at a time when many traditional industries are suffering from decline and labor shortage means that workers need not be displaced, and automated production, blockchain logistics, and stores without cashiers can proliferate without the societal upheaval and friction that is so often feared. At the same time, the digital transformation is opening new avenues for Japanese industry to compete. Globally, new technologies create new markets that allow for business growth and productivity gains. Domestically, as companies pivot and reinvent, they have new demand for specific labor skills. This is happening just at a time when the looming labor shortage is increasing the bargaining power of labor, in particular the highest skilled segment. The new power relations are allowing employees to renegotiate the time-honored institutions of Japanese labor relations.

When hearing about the ageing society and the digital disruption, most people conjure up images of a cute-looking robot helping an elderly person with a daily chore. Indeed, Japan is often said to be a leading innovator around robotic applications for nursing and "silver" entertainment.[5] However, in this Element we look at something much broader and deeper. The digital transformation is much more than just an increase in robots, or even the interaction between robots and society. It is about a fundamental shift of economic activity, a deep-seated transformation of what sectors of the economy perform what types of business, how production is governed, how productivity is measured, and how goods and services are presented and consumed.

---

[5] "Robots take part in Japan's elderly care," *CGTN*, June 30, 2019; "Aging Japan: Robots may have role in future of elder care," *Reuters*, March 27, 2018.

For business, this necessitates a complete "model change," as Toyota CEO Akio Toyoda labelled it.[6] For society, this means a redefinition of self, privacy, and lifestyle, as well as a shift from owning things to consuming subscription services, and to working in fully automated settings and moving in automated systems, with constant connectivity and information updating. For government, the digital disruption requires a redesign of regulation and policymaking in a world governed by ubiquitous connectivity, immediate information sharing, and borderless competition. Japan's social contract – the tacit agreements of the rights and responsibilities of business, people, and the state – is also being rewritten. This means, Japan's entire political economy is in the process of being updated for the "society 5.0" version. The twin disruptions are occurring with certainty; they cannot be avoided. This leaves the government with no choice but to adjust to the shifting industrial and societal architecture.

Japan's rapid economic growth after WWII was characterized by proactive "industrial policies" that consisted of the rank-ordering of industries and anointing of champions to streamline growth through within-industry coordination. The digital transformation is now shifting the global technology frontier to places that the state can no longer organize or coordinate. For companies, the need to compete in the global race for deep-technology advances necessitates new business strategy. For the state, industrial policy needs to be redesigned to support corporate strategies that transcend industries and even economic sectors, as the overall governance of Japan's markets evolves. In 2020, Japan was the first country to appoint a "Minister of Digital Transformation" *(Dijitaru kaikaku tantō daijin)*, to design a Digital Agency (*Dijitaru-chō*) within the government tasked with bringing about a reorganization of ministries, responsibilities, and policymaking processes.

As of 2022, hardly a day goes by where the "digital transformation" is not front-page news in Japan. As this term is unwieldy, especially in Japanese *katakana*, it has been abbreviated as the "DX." We will adopt Japan's term of "DX" here, to refer to this coming technology–society–strategy shift in its entirety. In the United States, even though the "digital transformation" is still spelled out, new vocabulary has emerged to describe the coming industry-specific disruptions, often as a portmanteau ending with "-tech," such as fintech (financial services), insurtech (insurance), agrotech (agriculture), proptech (real estate), matech (marketing), or medtech (health sciences and medical devices).

The goal of this Element is to lay out how the combination of the DX and demographic change are changing the underlying logic of Japan's political

---

[6] "In search of Akio Toyoda's successor: Toyoda wants a new culture," *Automotive News,* April 15, 2019.

economy, through the upheaval of the country's industrial architecture and employment patterns. We show how industries such as agriculture and the manufacturing sector are evolving, and how the DX is affecting employment, skill formation, and education. Existing assumptions and definitions regarding how to divide economic activity into sectors, or how to assess policy successes, are no longer meaningful as the evolving business models straddle sectors and the technology race is global. The DX reduces corporate resource dependence on the state and empowers businesses with deep technology expertise. The COVID-19 pandemic has only accelerated these shifts, by pushing forward work style changes, shifting career ambitions, and the phasing out of legacy business sectors. In the new political economy, neither business nor people nor the state will work as they used to.

As the first country to face the onset of demographic change, Japan becomes a trailblazer. Its experience may shape how other countries utilize the DX for domestic social policies, and its mistakes may prove relevant for others. As the third-largest economy in the world and a leader in advanced production technologies, materials, mechatronics, and system solutions, Japan has the resources to be a strong global competitor at the technology frontier that is the manifestation of the DX. In what role and with what capacities the Japanese state will emerge, and how Japan's political economy is preparing to compete is likely to be once again an important case study.

We focus on the opportunities that the twin disruptions are opening up for Japan. Of course, the DX will create similar opportunities for Japan's global competitors, and it is unknown who will win in the jockeying for position at the technology frontier, or who will dominate the global supply chains of the future. Within Japan, too, there will be losers. These will include large firms that fail to adapt, and small firms and other parts of society that are left behind in low-productivity parts of the economy. To what extent these are stuck will depend on how the state will be able to compensate them, and how companies will adapt and reskill. The "lucky moment" may create new opportunities for the state to minimize some of these costs, as we allude to in Sections 5 and 6. That said, we will focus on the DX change process and the new constellations that are emerging. A study of the social costs as well as the role of small firms in Japan's DX is beyond the scope of this Element and left for future research.

Our discussion will be structured as follows. We understand "political economy" to mean the interplay between business, people, and the government. We will analyze their relationships in three main sections in this Element.

For *business*, we are interested in how companies are adjusting corporate strategies for deep-technology innovation and business models that embrace servitization. The DX will require new skills, new specialization, and new approaches to innovation and measures of profitability. Japan's leading companies are redefining their core businesses and identities to become providers of deep-technology solutions.

We use the label of *people* to refer to demographic change and the labor shortage, as well as changes in Japanese employment practices.[7] The DX will require new designs and processes in education as well as the reskilling of the current workforce. Further, the newly emerging job mobility has begun to alter the rights and responsibilities of employers and employees, just as the DX is removing old jobs and creating new ones.

The role of the *state* is also changing as the government no longer has the answers in a VUCA (volatile, uncertain, complex, ambiguous) world. Power relations between politicians and bureaucrats have changed, old industrial policies no longer apply, and fewer young people are applying to government jobs. But the DX is also bringing new tasks for the state, from geo-economic strategies to protect Japan's global production networks, to education, retraining, and intellectual property protection.

We begin, in Section 2, with an introduction of definitions, examples, and basic data on the DX and demographic change. Section 3 offers context with a succinct summary of Japan's post-WWII political economy, as needed to appreciate the transformations analyzed in this Element. Sections 4, 5, and 6 look into the actual DX that is underway, by presenting detailed case studies on evolving business strategies, employment patterns, and state policies. Each section presents examples of how the DX has already impacted Japan. Section 7 concludes that the "lucky moment" gives each of the three pillars of Japan's political economy a push toward finding a new identity. Whether Japan will be successful is unknown at the time of this writing. Most likely, mistakes will be made, strategies will get thwarted, and losers will suffer. But good or bad, Japan's experience will soon repeat across parts of Asia, followed by Europe. How Japan prepares, and how we can best analyze and assess Japan's progress, will be meaningful for many other countries.

2 Definitions: The Digital Transformation (DX) and Demographic Change

This section introduces the core concepts we will discuss, to set up the case studies of ongoing change and transformation. To illustrate the ground-shifting

---

[7] The study of people as consumers and the adaption of new technologies is a separate research agenda that requires tools and frameworks from sociology and psychology. We leave this topic to future research.

impact of the DX, we begin with a glimpse into the future of the automobile industry, which is morphing from a manufacturing into a "mobility-as-a-service" (MaaS) business. We then present our argument for why the DX is inescapable, an analysis of what the DX means for Japanese business, and data on demographic change in Japan.

2.1 Vignette: The Automobile Industry of the Future

Imagine it is the year 2030. Like most other people, you no longer own a car. Instead, your transportation needs are filled through a monthly subscription service, similar to how Spotify or Netflix answers your audio-visual entertainment needs today. For a monthly fee, you are assured the provision of just-in-time mobility services. When you need to go somewhere, your phone presents you with a menu of transportation modes. Your choices may include a self-flying automobile for a short hopper, or a car that is parked in your immediate vicinity and will arrive promptly. This could be either electric, solar, or hydrogen-powered. It will be self-driving, and quietly and expeditiously take you to your destination.

If you think that 2030 is too soon for this utopian scenario to materialize, note that some of these options already exist, such as the German corporate car-sharing company *fleetster*, or Zipcar in the United States. In fact, the Toyota Motor Corporation – the world's largest auto maker in 2022 – expects all of this to materialize much sooner. In 2019, Toyota launched "KINTO," a subscription service car company, as well as "Toyota Share," a car-sharing service.[8] In April 2021, Toyota acquired Lyft's self-driving unit, to enhance its existing "e-Palette," a self-driving, battery-powered electric small bus that was launched to transport athletes and visitors to and from venues during the 2020–1 Tokyo Olympics.[9] Earlier, in 2017, Toyota had invested $400 million in a group of Tokyo-based Japanese engineers who were moonlighting on a flying car project. In August 2020, their company, SkyDrive, Inc. made its first safe "test fly" in Aichi Prefecture with a three-wheeled drone that can carry one person. Of over 100 global flying car projects at the time, SkyDrive was one of only a few to take off and land safely.[10] To double down on its bets on the flying car, in 2020 Toyota invested another $400 million in Joby Aviation, a California-based

---

[8] Toyota Annual Reports of 2018 and 2019, https://global.toyota/en/ir/library/annual/

[9] Toyota website, www.startyourimpossible.com/en-us/mobility; https://global.toyota/en/news room/corporate/29933371.html; "Toyota to buy Lyft unit in boost to self-driving plans," *Reuters,* April 27, 2021.

[10] "Toyota eyes flying car future," *Industry Week,* May 15, 2017; "Japanese flying car startup aces driver test," *Observer,* August 28, 2020. Toyota's main competitors in 2020 included Hyundai, Airbus, a JV between Porsche and Boeing, Uber, Google, and possibly Apple, and startups companies such as eVolo (Germany) and EHang (China).

startup company. Its eVTOL (electric, vertical take-off and landing) machine looks like a small helicopter but with six horizonal rotators.

These efforts are all in pursuit of a new corporate vision for Toyota to become the world's leading MaaS provider. Toyota aims to dominate an industry that will morph automobile manufacturers into transportation operators of electric, self-driving vehicles and drones. This will represent a complete identity change for Toyota as a company. In the 2010s, Toyota earned annual revenues of about $250 billion by selling roughly nine million cars globally. Now, Toyota envisions a future where it no longer sells cars at all.[11] It may still make cars, flying and otherwise, but they will constitute the Toyota rental fleet that offers on-demand transportation and other services.

Traditionally, car companies have been designers and assemblers that oversee a large supply chain of part makers. The assembly process is complicated and characterized by significant economies of scale (Womack et al. 1990). As we will see in more detail in Section 4, "industry 4.0" now brings a shift to digital manufacturing that dramatically alters the logic and economics of production. In addition, in this shift to MaaS the design and product characteristics of a "car" are also turned upside down. Traditionally, car companies have competed with style, design, and engineering, all on a spectrum ranging from high-quality workmanship to low-price affordability. But in a future with no personal ownership, markers such as status, brand, looks, or engine (or motor) size will soon be irrelevant. Instead, going forward, the vehicle itself will become standardized and commoditized. This will be necessary in order to strip it of any idiosyncratic complications and make it as user-friendly and interchangeable as possible for the shared economy.

Add to this "servitization," that is, the creation of business models based on revenue generation from subscriptions and other platform offerings. Until now, car maker services have consisted of leasing and repair services offered through dealerships. These were often seen as a necessary by-product of the core business of manufacturing.[12] Going forward, transportation services will be the new core business, and add-on service offerings will provide differentiation from competitors. Such offerings may include in-vehicle entertainment options, well-being programs, concierge and shopping services, and of course, user data collection.[13]

---

[11] Toyota Annual Reports of 2018 and 2019, https://global.toyota/en/ir/library/annual/; Toyota investor relations website, https://global.toyota/en/ir/financial-results/

[12] METI (2018b, 2019a), and www.emeraldgrouppublishing.com/topics/blog/what-servitization-manufacturing-a-quick-introduction

[13] Toyota's 2019 "Connected and MaaS strategy" had three components: a mobility service platform for transportation, big data processing for traffic optimization, and additional mobility and daily-life services. "Toyota's connected and MaaS strategy," presentation, February 6, 2019, https://global.toyota/pages/global_toyota/ir/presentation/2019_q3_competitiveness_en.pdf; Ryōsuke Izumida, "Toyota no MaaS senryaku, sekai de no genzaichi wa doko ka" (Where in the world will Toyota's MaaS strategy play out?), *Nikkei BizGate*, October 4, 2018.

Winners in the MaaS business competition will be those that offer the most immediate, reliable, and comfortable mobility solutions, at the best price. They will grow revenues with larger market share, which increases user data collection, which can be used or sold to marketing firms. That is, success will depend on how much traffic – literally and figuratively – the MaaS provider can attract to their platform.

Servitization will also bring a new meaning to the profession of the "car worker," which is shifting from a factory to a desk job. Employees of MaaS companies will have assignments ranging from IT and advanced operations management to logistics, mapping and data solutions, and designing and managing third-party offerings and alliances. Japan's shrinking workforce helps in this transition, as the labor shortage is already causing factory work problems. We will see in Section 5 how large companies are rolling out programs to "reskill" their existing office and shopfloor workforce. For younger workers, the government has launched an education reform, including the redesign of high school curricula as well as university course offerings to prepare the next generation of car workers for platform services jobs. For companies, the shrinking workforce leaves no choice but to retrain existing workers, and this affords Japan as a nation a chance to upgrade the skill level of its entire labor force. It also presents an opportunity to funnel the top talent into new and innovative assignments with fast-track promotions in ways that do not necessarily undermine the existing lifetime employment system.

The tectonic shifts in business models in Japan's car industry are but one example. They repeat across industries, as we will see in Sections 4 and 5. Automobiles have long been one of Japan's largest and most successful industries. Their pivot into a completely new business realm with different profit and employment logics is a harbinger of the changes that are to arrive for Japan's entire industrial architecture, which is being disrupted at the core.

2.2 What Is the DX?

The DX is much more than a replacement of people with machines. It brings tectonic shifts in economic activity, industrial organization, revenue generation, connectivity, and access to information. This shift is coming about thanks to recent rapid advances in technology, especially in data collection through connectivity, storage capacity, and computing powers. DX technologies are divided into hardware and software. The hardware infrastructure consists of advanced communication (5G), sensors and vision technologies, embedded communication tools in all buildings, systems, parts, and machines (the IoT, "internet-of-things"), edge computing devices (on-site data governance), and "the cloud" (data center governance). These new hardware capabilities in turn have triggered great advances on the software side, namely in the collection and analysis of data, including unstructured data such as video. The tools developed for "mining" (deciphering, sorting, analyzing) these scrambled data are labelled artificial intelligence and machine learning (AI/ML). In combination, these technologies disrupt how economies are structured, industries organized, companies compete, governments rule, and people work and communicate (METI 2017, 2018b, 2020b; Kimura and Numata 2018).

Despite the constant news coverage on these developments, as of 2022, many still wondered how soon the DX would truly arrive, and to what extent people would resist the intrusions into privacy that these shifts will mandate. Indeed, there were still few use cases to prove the superiority, or even basic utility, of some of these advances, such as bitcoin, blockchain, or flying cars. Some even claimed that AI did not yet exist beyond some basic levels of visual pattern recognition, or that as a matter of personal daily-life experience, infrastructure was not nearly advanced enough to even allow ubiquitous access to the internet. Inadequate cybersecurity was also becoming a major concern.

Yet, from the perspective of policymakers and strategy planners, in the public and private sectors, the DX is already a force to be reckoned with. It will arrive with certainty, sooner rather than later. Nearly all policymakers, around the world, have realized that they cannot afford to postpone preparations for a future that is sure to arrive and needs to be shaped to serve the national, societal, economic, and human interest. The DX has three salient features that make it a critical juncture for all countries, and will touch all actors and institutions of a political economy:

1) *Speed and volume* of information exchange. Whereas it used to take several weeks, days, hours, or minutes to transfer a few words across the world, information is now shared instantaneously. The volume of information transmittals is growing rapidly. Inventions spread faster and are adopted more rapidly. This can be exploited for good and sinister purposes, with potential for huge advances or conflict. For any domestic political economy, the arrival of the DX means that policy decisions can no longer rely on using "time" either as a competitive advantage or a regulatory delay to allow slow adjustments.

2) *Ubiquity.* The "internet-of-things" (IoT) means that every single thing, every machine, every input part, every household item, and every person – and even every pet – is constantly connected to everything else, generating volumes of data along the way. What seemed to be a science fiction movie just a few years ago is now reality; in this new world, a smart watch can talk to a refrigerator to

learn the expiration of the milk. There is no escaping this new interconnectivity, and no policy or strategy can be meaningfully upheld outside IoT.

3) *Borderless reach.* Breakthrough innovation used to be clustered in innovation ecosystems, such as California's Silicon Valley, where colocation of inventors, universities, and financiers facilitated the cross-fertilization of ideas. The DX means that access to latest advances and collaboration are shifting to the digital and transcend country borders easily. The COVID-19 pandemic has shown that geographic barriers to knowledge access can be overcome. Meanwhile, the globalization of value chains and the expansion of corporate global production networks, with complicated paths of transfer pricing, knowledge sharing, and supply chain management, all mean that the nature of competition is turning truly transnational. There will be winners and losers to the DX in all countries, and no state or business can withdraw from this new reality. For the state, this means that the benefits of domestic policy measures are easily diluted, and the nature of industrial policy needs to change if it is to support companies in this new global competition.

To remain relevant in this new fast, ubiquitous, borderless connectivity, businesses need new competitive strategies and skill formation processes, people must negotiate and adjust to new paradigms of work and private life, and governments need new policy designs. The COVID-19 pandemic accelerated these processes by forcing telework and related new technologies onto society. Fresh possibilities of interactions have been introduced, and existing patterns of communications challenged. In Japan, the high reliance on fax machines and personal signature stamps (the *hanko*) caused significant consternation and necessitated lockdown violations, while the United States rolled out vaccinations without the ability to track them in an online registry. Both caused chaos in different ways and highlighted the real implications of the VUCA world when practices and policies remain stagnant.

2.3 The DX and Business: Industry 4.0

For business, "industry 4.0" brings the advent of digital manufacturing, which will change not only the conceptualization of the shopfloor and operations management, but also the economics of efficiency. Digitization enables single-unit production and undermines the concept of economies of scale, and robotics will change the skill requirements for factory workers, as the future shopfloor foremen will mostly oversee the execution of computer programs. At the company level, the DX requires adjusting to the evolving global competition with a new vision and compelling strategy, as well as business models that exploit the emergence of new markets and forms of consumption. Many of

Japan's leading companies stand to benefit from the DX, given their long-standing strengths in manufacturing technologies as well as "deep-tech." This term was coined in the 2010s in venture capital circles, to distinguish "shallow-tech" inventions such as mobile apps, websites, and e-commerce services from more deep-seated, radical, and disruptive innovations. Deep-tech break-throughs require more time, and often address big societal and environmental challenges.[14]

2.3.1 Deep-Tech Japan

The most prominent deep-tech fields in the DX include advanced materials, advanced manufacturing, artificial intelligence, biotechnology, robotics, pho-tonics, electronics, and quantum computing. Global private investment in young companies working in those fields increased more than 20 percent a year from 2015 and reached almost $18 billion in the year 2018 alone. Large companies, including in Japan, are investing magnitudes more in R&D and acquisitions of cutting-edge technologies (BCG 2019).

To assess Japan's global competitiveness, Japan's Ministry of Economy, Trade and Industry (METI) has tracked market shares by Japanese companies in global deep-tech markets. A first study, in 2003, showed that many Japanese companies had relinquished market shares in global consumer end products, such as in electronics or household goods. But rather than a defeat, this can be viewed as a successful strategic pivot into deep tech. Schaede (2020) argues that this shift has enabled leading Japanese companies to focus on difficult-to-make, difficult-to-imitate technologies and thus compete against rising competitors in East Asia, in particular South Korea and China. It works because profit margins are much higher in upstream deep-tech areas: As long as the Japanese compan-ies do not stand still, they can sustain the high costs of technological innovation needed to stay ahead in the global competition. What is more, this specialized focus on innovating in upstream deep-tech segments makes Japan a key tech-nology player in the DX just as the DX is redefining the logic of production.

METI has since continued to collect market share data for a growing set of Japanese industries, from sensors needed for robotics, fine chemicals for elec-tronics, and advanced materials to AI technologies and flying cars (NEDO 2018). These survey data underscore that some of Japan's largest companies are global technology leaders in many important input materials and compo-nents. Figure 2 offers a snapshot of the breadth and depth of Japan's competi-tiveness, from car parts and medicine to advanced materials and components for electronics. The black bars (left-hand scale) show the estimated combined

---

[14] See www.bbva.com/en/what-is-deep-tech/

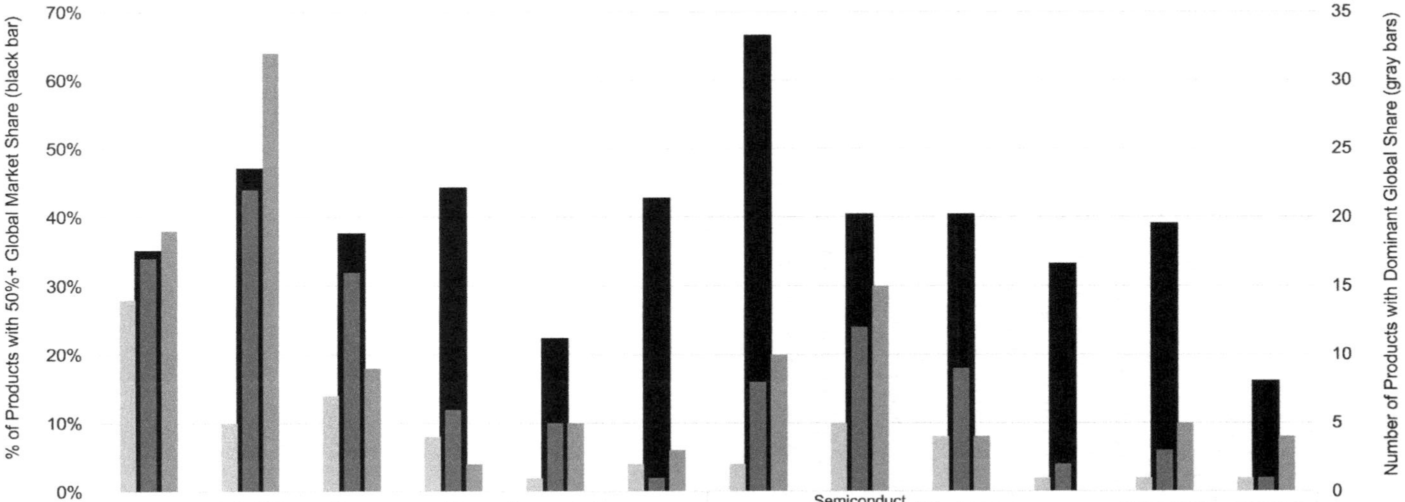

Figure 2 Examples of combined world market shares by Japanese companies in 2017

Source: Constructed from NEDO (2018)

	Automobiles	Industrial machinery	Home appliances	OA equipment	Communication on equipment	Instruments	Robotics	Semiconductor or components	Data storage components	Small motors	LED-related materials	Advanced materials
% over 50%	35.2%	47.2%	37.6%	44.4%	22.4%	42.9%	66.7%	40.5%	40.5%	33.3%	39.1%	16.2%
100% Market Share	14	5	7	4	1	2	2	5	4	1	1	1
75%-99% Market Share	17	22	16	6	5	1	8	12	9	2	3	1
50%-74% Market Share	19	32	9	2	5	3	10	15	4	0	5	4

market share of Japanese companies in that product category or industry, in percent. The gray bars (right-hand scale) are a visual presentation of the bottom legend rows. Overall, in this assessment of 1,217 product categories in 2017, Japanese companies combined to global market shares of over 50 percent in 309 categories (medium gray bars), and they held over 75 percent (dark gray) in another 112 products, and 100 percent in 57 products (light gray). In total, this added up to 478 products with dominant Japanese technology positions. Specifically, in 2017, Japanese companies dominated 66.7 percent of the input technologies needed for robotics, 47.2 percent for industrial machinery, 44.4 percent for office automation equipment, and 40.5 percent for semiconductors. Even though the end product may no longer carry a Japanese brand name, Japanese companies are important suppliers of the technologies that power these products.

The METI data are based on surveys and do not cover all industries, nor were those industry segments randomly selected. Thus, they represent just a snapshot and a lower boundary of the new shape and impact of Japan's competitiveness. The impression created here is supported by other studies. For example, a 2019 US study of industrial robotics and machine vision technologies confirmed that Japan's world market share exceeded 50 percent (compared to 30 percent in 2016). Competitors in this space included large firms (e.g., Denso, Epson, FANUC, and Kawasaki) as well as Japanese startup companies, such as Tokyo-based Connected Robotics, AI-company Preferred Networks, Paro Theropeutics, and Mujin, an industrial picking and sorting robotics company.[15] Overall, the message is becoming increasingly clear that a focus on end product market shares or brand names leads to a great underestimation of Japan's economic and deep-technology contribution to the world economy (Solís 2020).

2.3.2 The 2025 "Digital Cliff"

The fortuitous timing of the DX for Japan's political economy is also forcing change in an area where Japanese companies have come to be seen as pathetic laggards, namely: in software and the IT systems that run corporate Japan (e.g., Cole and Nakata 2014). In the early 2020s, most Japanese companies were facing a "digital cliff," that is, a tremendous challenge in their utterly obsolete corporate IT systems, both hardware and software that run operations ranging from supply chain and sales management to human resource management, finance, and corporate e-mail. In 2018, METI published a first report on this cliff, which estimated that by the year 2025, 60 percent of mission-critical IT

---

[15] "10 of Japan's top robotics companies leading the world into 2020," *RocketSpace*, July 24, 2019.

systems in corporate Japan will be so outdated as to be useless. The report also assessed that by 2025 Japan will need 430,000 additional IT specialists, and if no action is taken, this digital dilemma will cause economic losses of ¥12 trillion (roughly $120 billion) annually, or 2 percent of Japan's total GDP (METI 2018a, 2020b).

These deficiencies may come as a surprise: after all, were Japanese companies not at the forefront of IT in the 1980s? This is in fact the answer to the "digital cliff" puzzle: corporate Japan's IT infrastructure is now so outdated precisely because it was cutting-edge four decades ago. In the 1980s and 1990s, Japan was celebrated as the world leader in communication equipment, ICT/IT, and a numerical controls and mechatronics powerhouse (e.g., Prahalad and Hamel 1990). This leadership was deployed within Japan's traditional industry architecture of long-term vendor relations anchored on business groups. Almost all companies (as well as the government) outsourced their IT systems to one exclusive external vendor who built a highly tailored, customized system for each of their large clients. These company-specific software systems were installed on-premises, on customized mainframe computers. Over time, hardware and software were occasionally updated, becoming progressively more bloated, complicated, and outdated. Running on Windows 7 or even older, they were tied to ageing mainframes for which semiconductor firms no longer produced legacy chips. Due to the customized design, these systems could not be scaled or updated. And since the client companies typically did not view IT as strategically important, and managers were rotated through the IT division on regular intervals, companies eventually no longer understood their own systems. IT had turned into a "black box" (METI 2018a).

This situation poses a huge challenge for companies. Maintaining their idiosyncratic legacy systems eats up most of the IT budget, leaving little room for innovation. Nor can they attract young IT specialists, as no capable programmer would want to work on such antiquated systems. And, due to their ancient code, the legacy systems cannot be transferred or transposed to a current mainframe or into the cloud. METI blew the whistle in 2018, over growing concerns that even the country's largest banks and manufacturing firms were about to fall off this digital cliff as early as 2025 (Nishiyama 2021).

Perhaps ironically, the digital cliff offers yet another fortuitous window of opportunity for corporate Japan. Japanese companies must rebuild their entire IT infrastructure from scratch, just at a time when the DX is bringing new capabilities and cloud-based systems. New open-source and scalable IT infrastructures are likely to present corporate Japan with a new advantage, as it can leapfrog competitors who installed their systems a decade ago. It also provides an opportunity for Japanese vendors – including industry leaders NTT Data,

Hitachi, Fujitsu, and NEC but also a fast-growing corps of smaller independent providers – to revise their own business models. Instead of being confined by long-standing business group obligations that dictated customized solutions, these vendors now have an opportunity for more aggressive globally competitive positioning in the AI/ML era. As with other aspects of the DX, not all Japanese companies will survive the digital cliff. But those that do will then operate on a spick-and-span, up-to-date IT infrastructure.

2.4 The DX and People: Society 5.0

For the changes the DX is bringing for people, Japan's government has coined the phrase "society 5.0," defined as "a human-centered society that balances economic advancement with the resolution of social problems by a system that highly integrates cyberspace and physical space."[16] This refers to a new governance of society through constant connectivity and a revised definition of space and activity, from transportation modes to work styles (telework), health services (intelligent houses equipped with medical devices that send constant data to doctors for telemedicine), and fintech and blockchain (basing financial decisions on automated algorithms and enabling even large transactions in milliseconds). Of course, these innovations also raise major concerns, including privacy, personal record-keeping, and personalized medicine, as well as the future of jobs, learning, and skill formation.[17]

Society 5.0 is being rolled out before the rapidly changing demographic composition of Japan. Japan is the first industrialized country to experience both a rapidly ageing and shrinking society. Figure 3 shows that in 2020, 29 percent of Japan's population was over sixty-five years old, and this ratio is projected to reach 33 percent by 2035. This far exceeds any other country, as Japan ranks ahead of Germany, the United Kingdom, the United States, and South Korea, not only in the absolute level but also in the slope of the trajectory (Cabinet Office 2020a).

In addition to getting older, Japan's population is shrinking, due to a rising death rate and a fertility rate that has hovered at around 1.4 since 2005.[18] Assuming no drastic changes in fertility rates or immigration policies, Japan will remain a leader also in the shrinking workforce category, ahead of South

---

[16] Cabinet Office, "What is society 5.0," www8.cao.go.jp/cstp/english/society5_0/index.html

[17] The future vision of this lifestyle is being explored in various "smart cities" that provide next-gen housing, infrastructure, and energy solutions. Toyota's "Woven City" is a leading global example, www.woven-city.global/

[18] Deaths in 2019 hit a postwar record-high of 1.37 million people, with a record-high natural population decline of 512,000; www.mhlw.go.jp/toukei/saikin/hw/jinkou/suikei19/dl/2019gaiyou.pdf

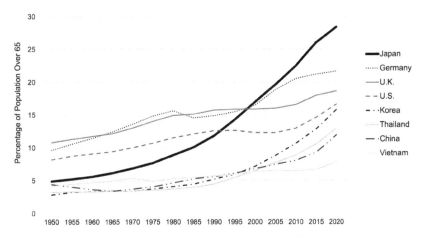

Figure 3 Ratio of population over sixty-five years old, various countries
Note: Legend is arranged in order of country ranking in 2020.
Source: Constructed with data from UN World Population Prospects, File POP/7–1: Total population, by five-year age group, region, subregion and country, 1950–2100

Korea, Germany, and Thailand. Figure 4 shows a projection through 2050, visualizing that Japan's workforce is predicted to shrink by at least 20 percent over the next two decades, from the current sixty-five million people in 2017 to fifty-two million by 2040.

Together, these trends mean that Japan's "old-age dependency ratio," which measures the number of people aged sixty-five and older per 100 people of working age, is higher than in any other OECD country. Just thirty years ago, in 1990, Japan ranked below OECD average with about 15 percent; in 2020, Japan topped the OECD with 50 percent, and is forecast to reach 80 percent by 2050 (OECD 2021). Within Japan, research on the future of society prepares for 2050, when the population is forecast to dip below 100 million (e.g., MRI 2021). This watershed is seen to exacerbate current trends of increased social dependency, falling productive potential, and an unsustainable domestic economy.

However, demographic change also brings novel opportunities, especially in combination with the tectonic shifts of the DX. Certainly, the DX is about to wipe out many traditional industries and jobs. For example, blockchain, logistics advances, and e-commerce are bringing a disruption that makes Japan's outmoded, multilayered wholesaling system superfluous. Fintech will eventually replace the physical bank, and with it the position of the bank teller.

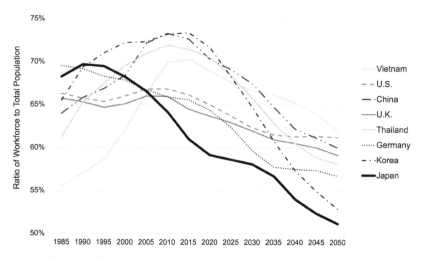

Figure 4 Workforce projection through 2050, various countries
Source: same as Figure 3

Agrotech is beginning to encroach on the old-fashioned tilling of farmland. But in Japan all of this is happening as wholesalers and farmers are, on average, sixty-eight years old and face difficulties finding successors, while local banks struggle to find business, and are about to be phased out (see Sections 4 and 5 for in-depth case studies). Thus, these sectors are poised for disruption just when the DX offers new solutions to provide and upgrade their economic functions and services.

The quantitative shift is only one aspect of Japan's demographic change. Qualitatively, too, Japan's workforce is undergoing a transformation, in terms of workstyle change, employment expectations, and skill specialization. A growing portion of Japan's next-gen workforce, and in particular the highly trained top talent, are displaying a different attitude in regard to work–life balance, the meaning of work, and the rights of employees vis-à-vis employers and coworkers, as well as meritocracy, individualized career planning, and upward mobility. To them, the lockstep promotions of the lifetime employment system (see Section 3) no longer seem attractive, and the looming shortage of such talent is increasing their bargaining power. They demand meaningful work content, and if unsatisfied, they are likely to explore new opportunities elsewhere.[19] In 2019, the government passed an encompassing "Workstyle Reform" law (*hatarakikata-kaikaku hō*) that specifically facilitates mid-career job-changing and greater employment flexibility.

---

[19] According to a 2017 survey, 35.7 percent of workplaces had hired mid-career employees. Ministry of Health, Labor and Welfare, www.mhlw.go.jp/toukei/list/dl/6-18c-h27-1-01.pdf

The DX also brings the need to reskill the existing workforce. With a shrinking workforce and continuing limitations on immigration, most companies will have to retrain their own employees to adjust to the technology shifts of the DX. As we will show in Section 5, Japan's youth score very highly in global math and science comparisons (OECD 2021), but education lags in workforce preparation. As such, the government has launched education reforms that address concerns that the country's education system is behind in basic computer skills, to prepare the future workforce for the DX.

These undercurrents for qualitative change in society gained high velocity with the 2020 onset of the COVID-19 pandemic. The sudden need to switch to distance learning as well as working-from-home not only boosted communication technologies and human acceptance of new modes of interaction. It also highlighted the deficiencies in Japan's education and office technology systems, forcing companies to make adjustments for at-home use of a work computer, the availability of VPN networks, and the role of printed documents and in-person deliveries in daily business. Perhaps most importantly, it further reframed the next-gen employee's mindset of what it means to work effectively and efficiently, and how they would like to structure their relationship with their employer.

These changes in business and demographics coalesce into a demand for a new role of the state. For example, rising labor mobility makes it uneconomical for companies to carry the responsibility for training the young, increasing the role of government to redesign, provide, and coordinate that service. Because the DX is fast, ubiquitous, and borderless, returns to capital are rising, as may inequalities. As the speed of change increases, the government needs to emphasize its role as a social protector. As we will recap in the next section, Japan's post-WWII political economy represented a canonical framework where employees got lifetime employment, companies got loyal employees and government protection, and the government got to coordinate and pick winners to maximize economic growth. The DX and demographic change have destabilized this quid pro quo. While it is not yet clear what the future may bring, the rights and responsibilities of business, people, and the state – that is to say, Japan's political economy – are evolving.

3 Context: Japan's Political Economy in the Post-WWII Era

To place our argument into context, we review here the main institutions of Japan's political economy of the post-WWII era. Our focus is on the quid pro quo between government, business, and people (in their role as workers), and the goals and coordination mechanisms of the government in spurring economic growth. In what was called the "developmental state" (Johnson 1982), the state designed a variety of mechanisms to coordinate industrial activity, guide technology imports, and streamline innovation. The state maintained this power by ensuring that almost all were compensated, including would-be losers. This worked as long as the pie was growing rapidly; as such, we also review the system's collapse in the 1990s, as the collapse after the bubble economy combined with the impact of deregulation to destabilize the postwar deal. The DX now brings an inflection point for the entire political economy as the core logic of the former quid pro quo no longer works for either state, business, or employees.[20]

3.1 Fast Economic Growth, 1950–1980s

After the severe losses in WWII, Japan as a nation sought to rebuild. The postwar economic recovery began with the export of basic supplies such as blankets to US troops during the Korean War (1950–1953). This brought the insight that the path to economic prosperity would depend on the successful commercialization of cutting-edge technologies. Japan's process of "catching up" could be accelerated if Japan could import foreign technologies, use them to design and manufacture new commercialized uses and consumer products, and then export these products into world markets. The higher Japan's value added in the design and manufacturing stages, the more foreign reserves were earned, with which more technologies could be imported, thus creating a virtuous cycle.

The critical elements in the upgrading cycle were the design of attractive commercial applications, continuous learning and improvement of manufacturing skills, and steep increases in product quality. Over time, this resulted in a core competence in *monozukuri*, "the art of making things," that is, the ability to manufacture large quantities of complicated products and materials with consistently high quality at high yields. Manufacturing companies extended their knowhow upstream to their suppliers, thus nurturing entire industry value chains domestically.

The government saw its role in accelerating this process through "industrial policy" (*sangyō seisaku*). This referred to the streamlining of development by way of coordinating industries and investments, fostering innovation and

---

[20] This section is a summary of Schaede (2008, 2020). For literature on the economic perspective of the developmental state and industrial policy, see Komiya et al. (1988), Patrick and Rosovsky (1976), Yamamura and Yasuba (1987), Ito and Hoshi (2021). For an analysis of business, see Abegglen and Stalk (1985), Dore (1973, 1986, 1987), Vogel (1979). For political science, see Anchordoguy (1989), Curtis (1988, 1999), Johnson (1982, 1999), Muramatsu (1981), Muramatsu and Krauss (1984, 1987), Pempel (1974), Vogel (2006). Haggard (2018) contains a deep bibliography and puts the developmental state concept into its regional context in Asia.

learning, and reducing duplicative effort and even competition, which were seen as potentially wasteful. The government rank-ordered industries and companies by relevance for the country's growth, and the cognizant ministries then designed roadmaps, including in terms of access to foreign technologies, subsidies and tax incentives, and export promotion schemes. In charge of manufacturing and therefore the most prominent ministry in this growth guidance was METI, the Ministry of Economy Trade and Industry (until 2001 named MITI, Ministry of International Trade and Industry).

The main purpose of industrial policy was to protect domestic infant industries to help them grow, and to promote exports in order to earn the foreign reserves needed for industrial upgrading. Domestically, companies were expected to grow in lockstep through "competitive convergence," that is, the large companies in most industries were incentivized to diversify in very similar ways, and over time very stable corporate hierarchies emerged (Porter, Takeuchi, and Sakakibara 1991). This stability facilitated the government's coordination efforts. For example, when Hitachi entered the nuclear power business, Toshiba followed suit. When Nikon developed a new camera technology, so did Canon. Corporate success was measured in terms of size and market share, and the largest companies had priority access to government promotions.

Export expansion was supported by allowing companies to adopt a "sanctuary strategy," whereby domestic price agreements allowed for higher profit margins that could then be used for aggressive pricing in foreign markets. The government allowed price coordination by exempting many industries from antitrust statutes, as well as enforcing rules fairly leniently (Schaede 2000, 2004). This oriented companies to compete in domestic markets through fast product improvements and customer relations, to justify high prices. Over time, Japan came to be known for super-high product quality, fast product life cycles, and excellent service. This was helpful in foreign markets as well, but there, competition was also based on price. Thus, companies used the domestic markets as a profit sanctuary, through retail price maintenance and other restrictive agreements such as exclusive retail chains. These profits were then used to sell at razor-thin margins into foreign markets, with the goal to capture global market share.[21]

The government's powers in coordinating industry rested on a large number of special laws. Some of these were industry-specific (e.g., steel industry law, communications industry law, large-scale retail law), while others were

---

[21] Foreign companies often could not compete, and some accused Japan of predatory pricing. One example was the US consumer electronics industry, which was wiped out in the 1980s (Schwartzman 1993). It remains unclear whether Japanese companies were indeed selling below cost, and to what extent US companies failed due to their own management mistakes.

encompassing, such as the "Foreign exchange and foreign trade law" (FEFTL, *Gaitamehō*, in short) of 1949. This law imposed restrictions on cross-border financial flows, which empowered METI (MITI at that time) to limit foreign investments into Japan and monitor the outflow of foreign reserves. The ministries used these laws to protect, incentivize, and guide industry leaders through a "carrot-and-stick" mechanism.

A second coordination lever was extensive financial regulation. A restriction on the use of bond and stock markets channeled most of corporate finance through bank loans. The 1949 "Temporary interest rate adjustment law" (TIRAL) tied most interest rates to the central bank's base rate, which enabled the government to guide the price for bank loans. Most of the time, this was used to keep the cost of borrowing low, in order to encourage private investment. This created excess demand for bank loans. The Bank of Japan, Japan's central bank, then employed tools of "window guidance," which referred to regular conversations with the largest banks, to nudge bankers to extend loans to the desired growth sectors and leading companies.

The champion industries evolved over time. Initially, great successes were scored in establishing fast-growing steel and shipbuilding industries, as well as chemicals and processing (e.g., refineries, rubber, ceramics, and pharmaceuticals) and heavy electric machinery (such as turbines, generators, and power plants). The 1973 "oil shocks" (OPEC price cartel), subsequent sharp increases in energy prices, and an environmental crisis required a pivot toward less energy-intensive, less polluting, high-technology sectors, including automobiles, electronics, precision machinery, and semiconductors.

Figure 5 shows the annual GDP growth rate (solid line, left-hand scale, in percent) and Japan's growing trade surplus (in bars, right-hand scale) from 1956 to 2019. The two decades of the early 1950s to 1973 were labeled the "period of rapid growth," when Japan recorded an average annual GDP growth rate of 10 percent, similar to China fifty years later. This growth rate halved after the "oil shocks," to an average of 5 percent. These successes also made Japan a trading nation: Beginning in the 1980s, the export push led to fast-growing trade surplus (vertical bars), and more than half of that trade was directed to the United States (Solís 2017).

By the 1980s, Japan's successes had resulted in a growing trade imbalance with the United States. This led the US government to launch a trade war to gain concessions for market access, deregulation, and voluntary export restraints. Trade negotiations lasted over a decade and turned increasingly acrimonious. By the mid-1990s, Japan had agreed to remove import barriers and trade controls; abolish restrictive financial regulation; remove most of the special industry laws; open the retail markets; and introduce more transparency into its

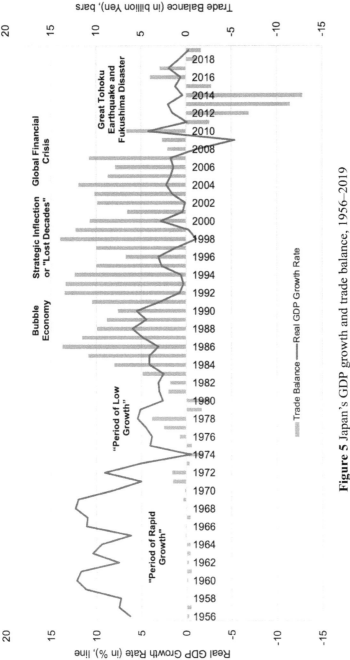

Figure 5 Japan's GDP growth and trade balance, 1956–2019

Note: Constructed with data from *Cabinet Office of Japan* (GDP) and *Japan Ministry of Finance* (trade)[22]

---
[22] www.esri.cao.go.jp/en/sna/data/sokuhou/files/2018/qe184_2/gdemenuea.html; www.customs.go.jp/toukei/suii/html/nenbet_e.htm

policymaking processes. But over time, these measures also eroded the government's levers in choreographing companies and industries (see Section 6). Overall, Japan's postwar system is generally seen as successful in ensuring fast economic growth, before the country lost its bearing in the 1990s, after the collapse of the bubble economy and the arrival of competition, especially from within Northeast Asia.

3.2 The Quid Pro Quo of Postwar Industrial Policy

Japan's postwar political economy was anchored on a social contract that is now under siege for having become too inflexible and too constraining. This tacit quid pro quo laid out the expected roles, rights, and responsibilities of the state, companies, and workers. The state's role was to enable speedy development by offering support to companies, ranging from low costs of borrowing to tax policies, subsidies, investment insurance schemes, and rescues in times of trouble. In turn, the state delegated a large portion of worker welfare to the large companies, in particular through offering stable, lifetime employment and benefits such as pensions. Corporate welfare was also extended to the many subcontractor hierarchies of these large firms. While expensive, companies could afford this assignment because corporate success was assessed by size, not profits (Schaede 2008). Over time, society came to expect that employment was a main component of corporate social responsibility (CSR) in Japan. Employees, for their part, were assured of stable jobs, steadily rising income, and stability. In turn, however, they had to trade in their rights to individual career planning as well as location and content of work, as the company could assign them to new rotations at will.

This setup allowed the government to greatly economize on social security, and those savings could be funneled not only into growth policies and infrastructure investments, but also into redistribution and the support of small firms outside the corporate network hierarchies, such as the services sectors and farmers (Calder 1988; Estevez-Abe 2008; Miura 2012). To this day, a large portion of Japan's social welfare is predicated on keeping companies in business, by offering tax breaks, subsidized bank loans, and other disbursements to small firms.

3.2.1 Business: Stability through Networks

This system created incentives and constraints for senior managers of large Japanese companies (for brevity, referred to here as "CEO," by which is meant the top managerial team) that were quite different from other countries. The key success metrics, in the eyes of the government and society, were growing sales and employment. Responsibility for lifetime employment and pensions meant that CEOs always kept an eye on stability and the company's longevity. Falling into distress or having to dismiss workers were considered the most egregious failures. In contrast, not being very profitable or having a low stock price were not considered nearly as problematic as long as the company was stable.

The "go-go years" of fast growth in the 1960s and 1970s offered many opportunities for growth, but the wide swings in the business cycle (as seen in Figure 5) also brought instability. And, because financial regulation strictly curtailed the issue of equity or bonds, companies depended on bank loans to finance corporate growth. In the 1970s, the average debt-to-equity ratio for large firms exceeded five, meaning their bank loans were five times the company's value. Failure to pay interest on these loans could easily topple the entire enterprise.

To reduce the risk of failure, many CEOs adopted a three-pronged approach. First, they continuously diversified into new businesses, including increasingly unrelated segments. At the time, corporate strategy advisers viewed diversification as stabilizing: having businesses with "uncorrelated income streams" under one roof was seen as safe, given that these business units were unlikely to all be hit by a demand shock at the same time. For example, Hitachi Co., Ltd., ended up as a manufacturer of trains, power plants, elevators, semiconductors, hard disk drives, refrigerators, chemicals, metals, and medical devices, among others. Nippon Steel ventured into amusement parks and semiconductors. Of course, adding more businesses also helped growing sales and employment. It also made the company "too big to fail"; that is, should it fall into distress it would need to be rescued to avoid large-scale unemployment and huge loan write-offs. Over time, however, this created huge conglomerates that became increasingly difficult to manage.

The second risk-reduction strategy was to join a business group (*keiretsu*) with stable, long-term trade relations cemented by cross-shareholdings. Many of these groups were vertical and included all core contributors to a product's supply chain. Lying on top of those vertical groups were six large, horizontal groups, which included roughly 200 of the largest Japanese firms as core members, and indirectly all their subsidiaries and suppliers. These groups formed mutual insurance schemes, by way of a tacit agreement that they all would be stable shareholders of each other, as well as trading partners that offered mutual support through purchases or trade credit during downswings. The cross-shareholdings also insulated companies from hostile takeovers, and corporate governance was left in the hands of internal executive managers and the main bank, while the shareholders were mostly group companies who were typically loyal and did not interfere with management (Lincoln and Gerlach 2004).

The third system stabilizer was the "main bank." Each of the six horizontal groups included a lead bank, which was the main provider of banking services and loans to all business group members and their affiliates. The main bank was also the "lender of last resort," in charge of rescuing group firms that fell into distress (Aoki and Patrick 1994; Hoshi and Kashyap 2001; Ito and Hoshi 2021). These tight intercorporate relationships helped spread the risk of bankruptcy across the horizontal business group. It also incentivized CEOs to heed long-term planning and collaboration in the domestic market. This system worked remarkably well: in the period between 1960 and 1990, fewer than 100 large, listed Japanese companies failed.

The biggest growth engine was to sell into foreign markets, and by far the largest and most attractive was the United States. Initially, the dominant strategy was to export made-in-Japan products through global sales offices, which were run as satellites with highly ethnocentric hiring practices, that is, all senior managers were Japanese, assigned to uphold headquarter culture around the globe. This focus on exports meant that domestic industrial policies were effective in also choreographing Japan's global business expansion beginning in the 1960s. It was only in response to the US–Japan trade war of the 1980s that Japanese companies began to build production plants around the world, to comply with local content rules.

Over time, US business executives and trade negotiators used the term "Japan Inc." to describe the thicket of intercorporate networks. The stable industry hierarchies facilitated industry policy, as it enabled repeated interaction and long-term reciprocal relations. But the system was still a market economy, and it allowed for mavericks and entrepreneurs. Even if not part of the master plan, underdogs could win and were often celebrated. Honda, Sony, Sharp, Nidec, Orix, all found ways to move up the ladder, and many suppliers managed to outgrow their roles, such as FANUC, Bridgestone, Denso, Nidec, and Hoya. An important route was their foreign successes. For example, Honda grew through motorbikes in Europe, while Sony captured the world with its transistor radio even before it earned respect within Japan. Thus, the domestic policy coordination was neither binding nor airtight, and it was counterbalanced by fierce competition abroad.

3.2.2 People: Lifetime Employment and Corporate Skill Formation

The Japanese people participated in the political economy quid pro quo in their roles as households, consumers and, of special interest here, workers. In post-WWII Japan, an estimated 75 percent of employees were in open-ended ("lifetime") positions, meaning they enjoyed job security, predictable promotions, and steady salary raises based on seniority, as well as on-the-job training and skill formation.[23] In return for this stability, they relinquished the right to determine their use of time, career path, and work location. This was necessary in a no-layoff system, so that the company had the flexibility to assign employees wherever needed. Regular employees were trained as generalists, promoted through the various corporate divisions, and assigned to divisions as needed. This resulted in job rotations abroad and overtime demands without regard to a worker's family situation or preferences, in ways that would have caused resistance in other countries. In the early decades, the trade-off was good for employees who valued stability above everything else (Abegglen and Stalk 1985). Over time, however, the system ossified, and when growth slowed in the 1990s, many employees were caught in a long-term struggle to find meaning in their jobs. The image of the "salaryman" as a hard-working, sometimes soulless soldier without agency became the fodder of movies and novels.

In the postwar system, companies assumed responsibility for employee training. While universities provided general education, corporate training provided applied skill formation and two-year, on-the-job training rotations. This resulted in a workforce deeply steeped in the operations of the company, but with few transferrable skills. Except for specialized engineers, the job market for mid-career employees was almost nonexistent. Society came to view job-changing as a failure, and there were few chances for upward mobility.

To this day, Japanese CEOs are usually promoted from within, working their way up through the rotations. A study of the late 1990s showed that 82 percent of senior managers in Japan had never worked for another company, compared with 28 percent in Germany and 19 percent in the United States; moreover, in the early 2000s, only 4 percent of Japanese CEOs were hired from the outside, compared to 20 percent in the United States and 25 percent in Europe and Asia (Waldenberger 2013).

The encrusted structures that this employment system created are now seen as Japan's biggest challenge to compete in the DX. Younger employees are no longer eager to commit to stable employment for security, especially as

---

[23] By the turn of the century this ratio had fallen to 65 percent. Nonregular workers were hired on limited-time contracts that could be extended, and they were paid less, without benefits. Two-thirds fell into the category of "part timers," most of whom were women reentering the workforce after raising children. For companies, part timers were a valve to flexibly adjust the workforce to the business cycle. With the labor shortage beginning in the 2020s, together with labor law reforms, companies began to reduce their reliance on nonregular workers.

opportunities abound in a labor shortage. Many salarymen find themselves stuck in companies past their prime, and this is seen as a loss to productivity and innovation. For CEOs, the challenge is how to shift from lockstep promotion and incremental progress to more diverse patterns that support breakthrough innovation, so as to compete with agility at the DX technology frontier. The matter of "corporate culture change" emerged as one of the management buzzwords around 2020.

3.2.3 The State: Coordination and the Elite Bureaucracy

In the catenation of industrial policy, the core government actors were not the politicians but the bureaucrats in the large ministries, in particular METI (MITI at the time), which orchestrated the guidance and coordination of private investment and production (Johnson 1982, 1999). Between the 1950s and 1980s, the Economic Planning Agency issued five-year plans that formulated growth goals. These were neither input plans nor output quotas, but guideposts to pave the way for the next cohort of "winning industries." But the bureaucrats did not rule by decree. Rather, the plans were negotiated with, and implemented by, the companies through their trade associations. Most policies were issued not as law but through guidelines. Because of the careful curation and industry involvement, there was usually little resistance. The occasional maverick faced ostracism by their peers as well as the ministry, which could prove costly in the long run.

Government–business relations were lubricated through a set of institutions based on interpersonal relations and repeated negotiations. The main channels were a multilayered network of trade associations, implementation through "administrative guidance" and voluntary compliance, and personal connections to ensure constant communication between ministries and individual companies.

Trade associations shaped and sanctioned industry policy directives. They were organized in a hierarchy from small, local, narrowly defined groups all the way up to encompassing umbrella associations to create various layers and platforms for industry representation and policy implementation. Trade associations shared information, coordinated their members, and punished the occasional mavericks. Their self-regulation ranged from collecting and sharing industry data to organizing price agreements (Schaede 2000). For the ministry in charge of an industry, this multitiered interest organization offered easy access to, and oversight of, each narrowly defined industry.

For implementation, the ministries often relied on "administrative guidance" (*gyōsei-shidō*), a type of "moral suasion" or "soft law." Buy-in was created through inclusion and nudging (i.e., the framing of policy options such that regulatees tend to voluntarily comply with the desired one). Lubricating these negotiations and facilitating the necessary flow of information were personal contacts between companies and their cognizant ministries. At the junior level, this was done through regular meetings between the bureaucrats and designated company employees. Over time, as these employees and bureaucrats were promoted through their organizations, these connections created thick networks of relationships between private sector employees and civil servants.

These connections were extended beyond retirement of the bureaucrats, which began at around age fifty-five. The retiring officials assumed new positions in the private sector, the associations, or other industry-based organization, and formed what was called an "Old Boy network," with "OB" used as an honorific term for an elder with influence (Johnson 1974; Calder 1989; Schaede 1995). These personal connections reinforced industry-based linkages, and further added to the "Japan Inc." image.

At the center of this coordination system was Japan's elite bureaucracy. Being in a position to draft the growth path for the country was an attractive profession that brought high status and esteem. Japan's smartest young men (rarely women until the turn of the century) were drawn into civil service. The entrance exam was seen as grueling, which created a superelite staff. The civil servants worked long hours at comparatively low pay, and were rewarded with power, status, as well as the highly lucrative postretirement positions.

The notion that the bureaucrats commanded the industrial policymaking process has been challenged by political scientists who see a larger role for politicians (e.g., Haggard 2018). Although the details of industrial policy were the purview of ministries, politicians were critical, of course, including in identifying policy measures that would appeal to certain groups of voters, such as farmers, shopkeepers, and other small firms. In the view of Calder (1988), the LDP managed to be reelected and stay in power for almost fifty years, thanks to its careful crafting of "circles of compensation." While the winners were supported and promoted, the losers were compensated in a myriad of ways, from exemption of antitrust statutes (e.g., retail price maintenance and cartels through small firm cooperatives) to subsidies and government-guaranteed loans even to failing companies.

Over time, the government–business connections and coordination mechanisms ossified. They were eventually viewed as harmful when scandals were revealed after the collapse of the bubble economy. How administrative reforms have evolved will be the topic of Section 6. For the context of our discussion here, the most important feature of the postwar industrial policy is that it was at its core domestic and industry-focused. We will see that the relevance of this type of guidance has been in decline for several decades, and with the DX it is approaching irrelevance.

3.3 The End of Postwar Growth: 1990s–2020

The successes of economic growth culminated in a four-year period of exuberant stock and real estate speculations in the late 1980s, referred to as the "bubble economy." Stepwise financial deregulation fueled aggressive lending and financial pyramid schemes, as banks, businesses, and bureaucrats lost their compass and engaged in increasingly irrational transactions. When the bubble imploded like a house of cards, it wiped out three times the size of Japan's GDP at the time in stock and real estate investments alone – a financial disaster of global historical dimensions.[24]

The various ways in which bureaucrats had coordinated industry were now viewed as enabling influence peddling and even corruption. A series of reforms around 1995 curtailed administrative guidance and OB retirements. The 1998 financial "Big Bang" reforms brought revisions of accounting and transparency rules (Toya and Amyx 2006). They also removed the restrictive foreign trade and currency rules, depriving MITI (renamed METI soon thereafter) of one of its strongest coordination tools. In the same year, the Ministry of Finance was stripped of its powers overseeing the financial industry, and the new Financial Services Agency (FSA) took over banking regulation. Financial deregulation allowed large companies to access foreign financial markets and pried open the domestic stock and bond markets. This lessened the large firms' reliance on domestic banks, and thereby eliminated the bureaucrat's core lever for picking winners. By 2000, the carrots and sticks wielded by ministries were largely blunted if not completely removed.

The collapse of the bubble economy brought a severe banking crisis in 1998, and a full-blown recession in the years 1998–2003. The economy fell into a twenty-year long period of low economic growth (see Figure 5). All efforts by the government to jump-start economic activity proved insufficient, from zero-level interest rates and fiscal stimulus packages to public works and generous grant programs for all parts of the economy. In combination, however, they raised Japan's government debt to 266 percent of GDP in 2021, the highest in the developed world. As economic growth remained elusive, the 1990s was labelled Japan's "lost decade," and the aughts were seen by many as a "second lost decade."

---

[24] For background, causes, and losses, see, e.g., Amyx (2004), Himino (2021), Hoshi and Kashyap (2001), Koo (2011), Shirakawa (2021).

Yet, in the background of this domestic economic malaise, Japan's largest companies were slowly yet steadily shifting their global business strategies. Whereas the direct postwar years had been anchored on export-driven growth, the 1980s brought a rapid increase in outbound foreign direct investment, that is, the location of production outside Japan (at the time referred to as "hollowing out," *kūdōka*). The trade war with the United States from the early 1980s to the mid-1990s further incentivized Japan's construction of a global production network, as the United States demanded "voluntary export restraints" by Japan's automobile and electronics companies. In response, Japanese manufacturers opened plants in the United States, Mexico, and Canada (to take advantage of the trade zone called NAFTA, now USMCA), and they took some of their largest suppliers with them. A new period began where corporate success is no longer measured in domestic market share, but profitability and technological leadership, and Japan's largest companies began to build a global production network to feed into global supply chains. By 2020, more than half of Japanese manufacturing sales were generated in plants located outside of Japan (see Section 4).

The turn of the century brought a sea change in the competitive dynamic in Northeast Asia, Japan's home turf. In the 1990s, Taiwan and South Korea had successfully caught up with Japan's mass-manufacturing skills, yet with much lower labor costs. This challenged Japan's leadership in consumer end products, especially in so-called white goods (kitchen electronics, such as fridges) and brown goods (audio/visual, including TVs). By the year 2000, Japan had also conceded semiconductor manufacturing to competitors in Taiwan and Korea. All three were then challenged by the rise of China as the "world's assembler." For Japan, on the one hand, the emerging China presented a huge and growing market just when domestic markets began to shrink, and lower labor costs also invited the move of production capacities to China. On the other, China was also a formidable up-and-coming competitor, just at a time when dramatic technology advances in logistics, freight, and communication brought the globalization of production value chains.

These events – deregulation, the collapse and recession after the bubble, and the new competitive setting – necessitated a wholesale shift in corporate strategy and business models. To compete with China, Japanese companies had to be not larger, but more agile, nimble, and smarter. Even Japan's largest, most diversified conglomerates could never be large enough to compete with China. This brought the onset of "choose and focus" strategies (Schaede 2008, 2020). Domestic stability insurance through business groups became less relevant, and financial deregulation since the 1980s had already greatly reduced the dependence on domestic banks. To operate at the technology frontier and always stay a step ahead of their fast-growing East Asian competitors, many of Japan's largest companies underwent drastic pivots. For example, Hitachi sold off most of its former businesses, to become a provider of advanced manufacturing service solutions as well as a competitor in smart cities and smart infrastructure.

For employees, the lost decades were a difficult time. Older workers were stuck in companies that were doing poorly. Perhaps worse, because many companies reduced their hiring due to the recession, many young university graduates in the 1990s and aughts were left out of the lifetime career path altogether. The rigidities of the lifetime employment system and its lockstep promotion meant those who started their working careers in nonregular jobs were unlikely to have a chance to become a "salaryman" later. The 1990s came to be called the "ice age of employment" (*shūshoku hyōgaki*) and initiated slow but ultimately monumental changes in how employees and employers viewed their mutual obligations. We will see in Section 5 how this created the setting before which employer–employee relationships are being redefined in the 2020s to suit the newly emerging needs of post-pandemic workstyles and the DX.

In response to these developments, the state also needed to adjust. The previous infant industry protection and export promotion had run its course. In Section 6, we will see that the new assignment is to support the leading competitors with vast global operations in an uncertain time, while also assuming new roles domestically in terms of compensating those left behind by the DX. For the country's technology leaders and reformers, the new VUCA world with its unknown technology frontier requires a new conceptualization of state guidance.

There is now a growing recognition that the 1990s and the early 2010s were not so much two "lost" decades, but instead the onset of a full-blown reorganization of Japan's industrial architecture and industrial policy. Many of the developments we analyze in the following three sections on business, people, and the state originated in this period, in a process of slow, careful, and methodical transition into a new era of competition. The DX is further accelerating these ongoing shifts to usher in the end of the institutions of postwar industrial policy.

4 The DX and Business: New Technologies, Industries, and Global Strategies

This section shows how the DX is bringing tectonic shifts to Japanese industry, thus shaping a new role for business in Japan's political economy. It showcases the examples of agrotech and digital manufacturing, to explain the technology advances that characterize the arrival of the DX. Since 1953, the ratio of employment in Japan's primary sector (agriculture, fisheries, forestry, mining) has declined from 43 percent to 3 percent today. Similarly, in the secondary sector (manufacturing, construction, electricity) it has dropped from a high of 40 percent in the 1970s to 24 percent today.[25] While this leads some observers to view these two sectors as increasingly irrelevant, nothing could be further from the truth. In fact, the DX and its innovations allow companies to give new meaning to these sectors, and to design business models that upend existing categories. Moreover, 50 percent of Japan's manufacturing revenues are now generated abroad, making advanced manufacturing and the management of global value chains central to how companies compete. Domestically, the DX is phasing out legacy industries such as multilayered distribution, which brings solutions to some of Japan's long-standing socioeconomic challenges as well as new opportunities for innovative companies.

4.1 Agriculture: The Making of a Twenty-First Century Tomato

Agriculture is usually considered the quintessential "primary" industry, and the starting point for a country's development. A decline in agriculture's contribution to GDP and employment is often celebrated as an achievement, namely, of development through industrialization. In this view, the image of the farmer is rarely flattering – someone tied to the land, with long working hours and strenuous physical labor, and business returns heavily influenced by the weather and natural disasters. Farmers naturally must aspire for their children to receive a good education so as to escape the hard, risky, and often unprofitable work of tilling land (Maclachlan and Shimizu 2022).

However, over the past decade a global turn to sustainable farming and organic food has challenged the world trade in agricultural products. "Farm-to-market" has become the buzzword not only of aspiring gourmet chefs and foodies but also environmentalists. Large-scale farming as well as meat operations and slaughterhouses are drawing growing concerns over unhealthy pesticides, fertilizers, and growth hormones, as well as ethics. Sustainable and responsible agriculture have become important signs of an advanced economy.

The DX is contributing to this shift by opening technology avenues to new types of agribusiness that address these concerns, from biotechnology to seed and soil optimization, artificial or lab-grown meat production, and advanced, AI-controlled fertilization, irrigation, and artificial lighting techniques. Rather than enduring hard work in the fields, the twenty-first-century agrotech farmer

---

[25] Calculated from Japanese government data, www.stat.go.jp/english/data/roudou/lngindex.html

is a university-educated expert in biotech and biomanufacturing, and a master of AI-assisted irrigation controls, aquaponic biochemistry, GPS spatial mapping, and UV light-assisted quality controls. This farmer is well-versed in overseeing fully automated production systems, including monitoring and fine-tuning complicated sensors and lighting installations, planting and picking robots, machine-controlled harvesting schedules, as well as autonomous sorting and grading machines.[26]

One component of this emerging agrotech sector is so-called vertical farming, that is, indoor farming in warehouses or high-rise buildings, under fully controlled conditions in many stacked layers, using artificial lighting instead of relying on the sun. By tuning the settings precisely to the needs of the plant and using soil-free growing techniques, vertical farming can achieve yields hundreds of times higher than conventional agriculture, all year round and with minimal herbicides or pesticides. The building may well be located downtown, in the immediate vicinity of markets, restaurants, and grocery stores, and the produce may reach consumers directly through e-commerce.

Vertical farming is revolutionizing global food production. In addition to freshness, this completely organic farm-to-market approach also promises higher product quality. It reduces the risk of contamination and the environmental footprint, as it reduces the use of water, electricity, and harmful chemicals. In 2018, the global vertical farming industry was estimated to have reached over $2 billion in revenues, and it was estimated to grow at about 25 percent over the next decades. While Europe was growing the fastest, the Asia-Pacific accounted for over half of global revenues in 2020.[27]

Japan is one of the world's forerunners in agrotech and vertical farming, and as of 2020 was home to the world's largest vertical farming company, Spread Co., Ltd.[28] Spread operates fully automated vertical farms in Kyushu and Nara, with daily lettuce production capacities exceeding five tons. In its multistoried buildings, robots take care of planting and harvesting, while fully automated cultivation processes optimize plant growth. Japan's industrial strength in energy-saving LED light technologies is bringing costs down fast, and companies like Spread are looking to expand their technology to more than 100 cities worldwide.

---

[26] MAFF is actively promoting "smart agriculture" to recruit young scientists into agrotech, with IT knowledge a key component of the job description, e.g., https://smartagri-jp.com/farmer/24

[27] Data from www.fortunebusinessinsights.com/industry-reports/vertical-farming-market-101958; see also blog on "Vertical farming – science fiction or the future of agriculture?" https://aucli mate.wordpress.com/2018/04/05/vertical-farming-science-fiction-or-the-future-of-agriculture/

[28] Company website, https://spread.co.jp/en/sustainable-farming/, and https://spread.co.jp/en/files/ news_20190624en.pdf

These production processes untie farming from location, weather, and seasons. Moreover, just as servitization in manufacturing redefines business models, farming is also expanding, including into packaging and farm-to-market logistics and sales. This has led Japan's Ministry of Agriculture, Forestry and Fisheries (MAFF) to label it the "sixth sector" – a Japanese-style play on words and math, to indicate that Japan's new agriculture business represents the sum of the primary, secondary, and tertiary sectors ($1 + 2 + 3 = 6$). And to boot, the association of agrotech with global warming, sustainability, and health affords the farmer new status as a critical contributor to balanced life and well-being in the New Economy.

One example of pioneering innovation in Japan's agrotech disruption is a sweet tomato called Amela, and its inventors and producers, Sunfarmers Co., Ltd.[29] In 1996, a team of researchers at a Shizuoka-based agriculture laboratory succeeded in cultivating a common Japanese tomato into a much sweeter type. Their breakthrough invention was an innovative type of soil called "coco-peat." Coconut husk fibers were found to optimize aeration and water retention, and also greatly reduce water waste. Sunfarmers named the tomato "Amela," a play on the local pronunciation of "isn't it sweet" (*amai*). Amela represents a new, replicable farming method for tomatoes that satisfies high standards for flavor, color, size, and sugar content. Rather than relying on a farmer's green thumb, Amela's growth is directed by AI/ML-controlled irrigation, temperature, lighting and CO_2 settings, and fertilizing schedules, meaning it gets better every day as its schedule improves. As greenhouse technologies advance, the future promises further energy savings. Not only is Amela sweeter and prettier than its peers, but it is also fully organic, with no variance, blemishes, or seasonality. As of 2020, Sunfarmers produced Amela in nine locations, all under the exact same settings. This has allowed fast brand promotion even though Amela carries a 100 percent price premium over a conventional tomato.[30]

How these tomatoes and other vertically farmed produce end up in the stores also represents another disruption, in this case of the political and economic institutions of Japan's postwar agriculture industry. Japanese farmers have conventionally sold most of their crops to the Japan Agricultural Cooperatives (JA), the umbrella association of local farming cooperatives. The JA then sells the produce through its own retail network, mostly as a price taker. Farmers have a certain income stability and carry neither marketing expense nor inventory risk, but in return they enjoy no upside revenue potential. Product

---

[29] Company website, www.amela.jp/; see Maclachlan and Shimizu (2021, 2022) for an analysis of the changes in the institutions and competitive forces in Japanese agriculture.

[30] Onedan Nōto, https://onedannote.com/19/

differentiation or quality are not highly rewarded in this system (Maclachlan and Shimizu 2021, 2022).

The DX now opens pathways to circumvent the powerful JA. Vertical farmers can equip their buildings with fully automated packaging machines and offer "farm-to-market" delivery to nearby stores and restaurants. Other direct-to-consumer sales channels include e-commerce, which promises high returns from setting up proprietary distribution channels and collecting consumer data for targeted social media marketing. All these afford entrepreneurial farmers extra opportunities to differentiate and become price setters. For example, in the case of Amela, Sunfarmers Co. operates an online shop for direct-to-consumer and direct-to-restaurant Amela sales, outside the rigid, JA-governed, multilayered distribution channels.

Amela is but a small tomato, and Sunfarmers continues to face formidable hurdles, given the high costs and technological intricacies of vertical farming. But this tomato's story represents a larger, and very important trend of shifting business boundaries and technology frontiers in agribusiness. Startup companies in Japan and globally are now entering the technology race in more complicated-to-grow produce such as rice, and meat such as Kobe beef grown in labs.[31] These innovations are expected to grow into massive global industries soon. A Japanese startup called Oishii recently discovered how to grow vertically farmed strawberries – and in particular, how to pollinate strawberries without polluting the indoor crop. In 2020, the "omakase berry" became a big hit and fetched a price of $10 per berry in New York, while Oishii attracted $50 million in A-Series venture funding and was hailed as "the Tesla of Strawberries."[32]

This focus on innovative technologies, higher yields, healthier produce and protein, as well as sustainability is happening just as Japanese farming is facing a significant ageing and shrinkage of its workforce, far exceeding Japan's already high national average. In 2020, the average farmer was sixty-eight years old.[33] A wave of impending retirements of the Shōwa-period (post-WWII) farmers, most of whom have no successors, is opening up new career opportunities in agrotech as a type of natural generational change rather than

---

[31] "Lab-grown meat is starting to feel like the real deal," *Science*, April 2, 2020; "Who knew high-tech farming of high-priced Japanese strawberries could be worth $50 million to investors," *TechCrunch*, March 11, 2011.

[32] Company website, www.oishii.com/, and "Vertical farming startup Oishii raises $50 million for bee-assisted, carbon-neutral strawberry cultivation," *AgTech Funder News*, March 11, 2021; "Meet Oishii, the Tesla of strawberries that could upend the $1.3 trillion produce market," *Biz News Post*, November 4, 2021.

[33] MAFF Statistics Related to the Agriculture Workforce, www.maff.go.jp/j/tokei/sihyo/data/08 .html

a displacement. Companies such as Sunfarmers face no labor shortage, as college graduates with science backgrounds are now drawn into vertical farming and its supporting industries, such as advanced materials, sensing, lighting, and AI/ML technologies.

All this is also challenging entrenched notions of Japanese farming as a mostly domestic business, justified by its contribution to self-sufficiency and sustained in exchange for votes. The productivity gains through agrotech mean that the future farmer will not need protection to compete. In fact, in 2019, the Amela technology was exported to Spain, where the tomato is produced in collaboration with a local cooperative.[34] Agrotech lends itself to the global cultivation of crops due to the fairly straightforward duplication of building design, automated production processes, and adherence to digital quality standards. Climate does not matter.

Perhaps the biggest new challenge for agrotech is intellectual property protection, as farming is no longer based on tacit knowledge but on copyable algorithms. Sunfarmers expended considerable effort convincing their counsel and bankers to think of Amela as a tomato in need of legal protection. This applies in similar ways to the breeding of and sperm trade in high-quality wagyu beef. Japan's Ministry of Agriculture, Fishery and Forestry is surely not the only bureaucracy in the world that struggles to keep up with the many innovations of digital farming. A series of seed theft cases in the 2010s underscored the extent to which the ministry is dependent on specialist input on such matters.[35] While it is not necessarily difficult to protect AI algorithms, a different regulatory framework is required to do so for agrotech applications.

All that said, Japanese farming is changing only slowly. Even as traditional farmers are exiting with generational change, the JA continues to control most sales channels. But even there new disruptions are looming, because new technologies for advanced logistics and distribution governance are beginning to attract a diverse group of novel competitors from other sectors. These range from IT companies NTT and Softbank (interested in e-commerce and user data collection) to trading companies Mitsubishi Corp. (and its Lawson convenience store chain) and Sumitomo Corp. (working with Ito Yokado and Seven-Eleven). Car maker Toyota has partnered with Jinmei, an entrepreneurial rice wholesaler, to invest in vertical farming-focused distribution, whereby Jinmei aims to be

---

[34] Company website, https://granadalapalma.com/index.php

[35] Author interview, Shizuoka, July 21, 2019. "Wagyū idenshi, ryūshutsu ni keijibatsu" (Theft of wagyu DNA materials to carry legal repercussions), *SankeiBiz*, January 20, 2020, and "Japan passes bill to protect intellectual property control for fruits," *Japan Times*, December 2, 2020. With this law, illegally taking seeds and saplings abroad can be punished with a prison sentence of up to ten years or a fine of $100,000.

a vertical rice grower and Toyota is keen on rolling out its brand-new fleet of self-driving trucks, to explore new possibilities for its smart city concept (as seen in Section 2). All these are examples of how agriculture is spilling over into other sectors and industries, and how emerging technologies are turning agro-business into the "sixth sector."

4.2 Traditional Business Upgrading: Ageing and the "Gracious Exit"

The DX is also bringing upgrades to outdated domestic business structures in the other sectors. Not just in agriculture, but also in businesses ranging from simple construction to lower-tier manufacturing suppliers, wholesale distribu-tion, small-store retail, and even the taxi industry, the DX is disrupting old-fashioned structures that are known to be inefficient and in dire need of reform. It is here where the simultaneous arrival of the DX with demographic change creates one of the more visible "lucky moments" for Japan.

Just as agrotech is filling the impending void caused by the rapidly ageing farmers, DX technologies are replacing other old-fashioned sectors that are on their way out anyway. For example, blockchain is revolutionizing logis-tics just as Japan's wholesale businesses need to be restructured, smart (digital) construction is enabling unmanned operations, and digital manufac-turing is replacing low-level contractors who cannot find successors. While replacements of this sort are a major threat to job security and societal stability in many countries, for Japan the DX is offering a welcome solution to low productivity and the growing challenge of the so-called "succession problem."

A 2020 study by Teikoku Databank found that the average age of Japanese CEOs was 59.9 years for all companies, but in small firms (with sales of less than ¥100 million, or about $1 million), 28 percent of CEOs were older than seventy. Figure 6 visually presents this trend, by graphing the age distribution of small-firm CEOs in Japan over the past three decades. Whereas in 1995 (lowest, dotted line) the distribution peaked at fifty years old, by 2018 the peak had moved to over seventy years old.

Many of these CEOs founded their small firms in the 1950s and 1960s and have run them ever since. Their major challenge is to find a successor: When the company possesses few valuable assets, or operates in a rapidly declining sector, even the founders themselves can hardly blame their children for pursu-ing a different career. The labor shortage and the allure of novel DX jobs in emerging sectors further exacerbates the talent drain on traditional businesses. As such, the ageing trend and succession challenge in small firms are forecasted to accelerate rapidly, with many firms simply unable to continue.

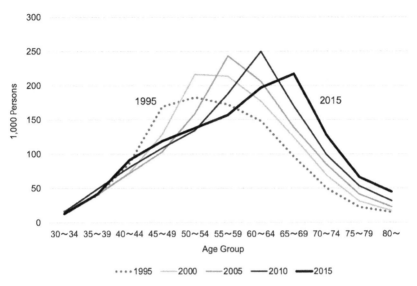

Figure 6 Age distribution of small-firm CEOs in Japan, 1995–2015
Source: Constructed from www.chusho.meti.go.jp/pamflet/hakusyo/H30/h30/excel/
b2_6_02.xlsx

A large portion of these very small firms are neither competitive nor profitable. However, instead of allowing market forces to bring about bankruptcies and layoffs, which would cause embarrassment and necessitate social security payments, Japan's government has long chosen to offer financial loan programs even to completely unproductive firms. The purpose is to provide loans until these firms can be "graciously phased out" through attrition, thereby preserving the dignity of founders and their employees who can uphold the appearance of productive work.[36] The increasing age profile of founders means that this inflection point is near. This makes the timing of the DX fortuitous, as the technology advances can facilitate exits and help upgrade the declining industries, just at a time when their founders are about to retire. The social disruption remains limited, and the industry overall can expect huge productivity gains.

The wholesale/retail industry is an example of a sector that is now at this transitional "lucky moment." According to the "Economic Census" of 2019, there were a total of 400,000 companies in this industry (until 2016, all sales offices were included in the count, resulting in a total of 1.36 million companies, of which 368,000 were wholesale offices). In either calculation, 99 percent of

---

[36] Interview with a Japanese executive, Tokyo, March 2018, who described this as the typical approach of Japan-style restructuring: "You know how this works in Japan, it doesn't get shut down but is phased out graciously, through attrition. We wait until most employees are retired, then we close it."

companies had fewer than five employees, and these 99 percent account for less than half of total industry revenue.[37]

From the 2016 data on 368,000 wholesalers, it was estimated that roughly two-thirds were "middle layers" who traded only with other wholesalers. This reflects Japan's antiquated, multilayered distribution system, where a small item – such as a six-bottle case of beer – would make its way from the very large-scale brewery to a large wholesaler, from there to a regional one, then onto a smaller truck for a specific area, and from there off on a light truck for daily delivery to a specialized, small neighborhood liquor store. Standard explanations for these many middlemen included geography (winding, narrow roads), small shops and the need for frequent deliveries, shopping habits (small houses, small refrigerators, and shopping as a social event for housewives), and the sheer political power of players in the distribution system due to their large numbers, and resulting supportive policies such as property tax deductions for turning one's house into a store (Patrick and Rohlen 1987; Larke 1994).

Today, both the demand and supply for this distribution system have drastically changed. As houses have grown larger, more people have cars, and more women work, the daily shopping in the neighborhood has been replaced with a once-a-week trip to a large supermarket, to economize on time and price. Deregulation of rules for large-scale stores in the 1980s and 1990s further facilitated this once-a-week shopping. For daily needs, ultra-efficient convenience store chains have penetrated the neighborhoods (Tanaka 2012). The tiny local greengrocer is no longer needed, and deregulation has also long weeded out specialized liquor and rice stores.

In their stead, on the supply side, blockchain, drone-based deliveries, and other swift advances in logistics will soon take over and replace the many middle layers of this convoluted distribution system. The gracious exit of these middle-tier distributors and the small stores they serviced will bring huge efficiency gains to Japan's economy. In contrast to the perceived destruction often associated with automation and disruption, for Japan the DX can well be a solution, not a threat to society.

4.3 Digital Manufacturing and Edge Computing

In addition to solving structural problems of low productivity sectors, the DX is also presenting new opportunities to compete for Japan's leading large companies. Given Japan's core competence in "*monozukuri*," mechatronics, factory automation, and robotics, it is no surprise that its top manufacturing companies –

---

[37] Calculated from www.e-stat.go.jp/dbview?sid=0003414037 and www.meti.go.jp/statistics/tyo/syougyo/result-2/h26/xlsx/kaku1.xlsx

together with competitors from Germany – are at the forefront of advancing digital manufacturing. Also referred to as "industry 4.0," this brings a novel manufacturing paradigm in which all machines and parts are interconnected with sensors and wireless connectivity, so that production can be fully programmed, and all parameters are known at all times.

Of course, today's factories are already quite automated, but digital manufacturing is a huge jump from the existing production pyramid with its five levels of unconnected planning software systems. Once an entire shop floor is equipped with 5G wireless bandwidth and all parts with built-in sensors, robots can oversee the entire production process in one unified system that is constantly optimized and improved through machine learning. Countries and companies differ in the speed with which they can upgrade legacy shopfloors with 5G-equipped ones, or build entirely new factories. But even though the timing is in the future, the new dominant design of the core features of an "industry 4.0 shopfloor" is already established.

"Industry 4.0" brings two huge disruptions to manufacturing. The first pertains to the flow and speed of manufacturing and the management of production processes and supply chains. Because machines do not need to eat, sleep, take vacation, or negotiate pay, there is little need for downtime. And, advanced sensor and real-time communication technologies enable the manufacturer to know where all parts are at all times. This complete information and transparency, also in blockchain-based open ledgers for supply chains and parts logistics, is about to perfect the operations management design of on-demand, just-in-time production and deliveries.

The second is that it upends what we know about the economics of manufacturing. The "industry 4.0" machine can switch over to making a different product with just the push of a button. This makes single-piece or small-batch production almost as efficient as mass manufacturing. This augurs the end of the conveyor belt line and, eventually, the logic of scale economics, and is about to revolutionize operations management and product design (Holst et al. 2020).

What is more, on a 5G-equipped and fully connected shopfloor, all parts or end products in a factory have a "digital twin." This is a file that sits in the cloud and monitors the part's or product's performance through its lifetime, in real time. Not only does this allow ongoing, continuous product and production optimization by the manufacturer. Users, too, can always know whether their product needs repairs or updates. To make this more concrete, imagine a time when your product – be that a refrigerator, computer, or car (if you will still own one) – never breaks down, because the condition of all parts and components is known in real time and you are alerted of the need to repair before anything breaks. Perhaps more importantly, the same will be true for airplanes, trains, medical equipment, and nuclear power plants.[38]

On the "industry 4.0" shopfloor, robots and machines are in constant communication with each other, and with all parts. Although digital twins and key metrics are stored in the cloud, most shop floor activities are orchestrated locally, in what is called "edge computing." This refers to the computation of information and immediate orderissuing, as well as data storage and encryption security not in the cloud, but at the location of the action (called *gemba* in Japanese). In technical terms, edge computing is a "distributed computing framework that brings applications closer to data sources such as IoT devices or local edge servers."[39] This proximity to data at the *gemba* brings faster data capture and response times and frees up bandwidth for the cloud. Eventually, there will be an edge server in every car, building, factory, and other locations, to govern the *gemba*-specific, immediate control needs.

One company at the forefront of edge computing is the Mitsubishi Electric Company (MELCO). Its pole position is reflected in the fact that its engineers were recently counted among the highest-paid Japanese executives, due to rewards for their inventions. Since 2017, Japan's listed companies have had to disclose all executive pay exceeding $100,000 in their annual reports. From those reports, media have created the so-called $1 Million Club, a ranking of the highest paid businesspeople in the country. In 2018, there were 704 such people, and many were surprised to see that 22 were from MELCO. Normally other Mitsubishi Group firms would report higher salaries. What is more, MELCO is a Japanese electronics company, an industry often seen as having collapsed since the heydays of Sony and Panasonic in the 1980s. Yet, in 2018, MELCO researchers made discoveries so significant that their individual bonuses propelled them into the group of highest paid businesspeople in Japan, one of which was "fast real-time control responses and cipher algorithms" for data security.[40] This is but one example of how, behind the scenes, a quiet yet powerful transformation of leading Japanese companies – in this case, in electronics – into DX competitors is taking place (Schaede 2020).

In 2020, MELCO had 146,000 employees and annual revenues of around $44 billion.[41] The company looked back on a 100-year history, during which it has morphed from a maker of electric fans, hydraulic generators, elevators,

---

[38] Author interviews, Tokyo and Aichi (Japan), Boston (USA), and Darmstadt (Germany) with policymakers, engineers, robotics specialists, and CEOs, 2018–2019; see also Schaede (2020, ch. 10).

[39] www.ibm.com/cloud/what-is-edge-computing

[40] www.news-postseven.com/archives/20181203_815650.html

[41] In 2021, MELCO was embroiled in an inspection data deceit scandal in several air conditioner and train parts divisions. While this was a huge setback and led to the CEO's resignation, the

escalators, and radios in the pre-WWII years to a postwar leader also in air conditioners, radar and satellites, machine tools, color TVs, LCD screens, and critical components for trains, cars, and power plants. The company diversified further, and in the 1980s commanded a brand name also in household devices (air conditioners, humidifiers), computers and mainframes, lasers, oscillators, and semiconductors. The end of the bubble made the 1990s a difficult decade for MELCO, and eventually the company withdrew from many of these former businesses. In 2001, MELCO's mobile phone 3GPP encryption technology won a global competition to establish the world cipher algorithm standard. The winning factor was the high quality and small size of the algorithm, which is now installed on all cell phones worldwide.[42]

Since the early 2000s, MELCO has slowly but steadily pivoted into becoming a leader in edge computing. The focus is on the three existing core businesses of (1) large building electric infrastructure (air, light, elevation, security), (2) automotive components, and (3) factory automation. Edge computing technologies now allow MELCO to turn these three into offering (1) smart solutions for security and controlled settings in office buildings and hotels, (2) fast-reacting self-driving cars and autonomous systems, and (3) digital manufacturing solutions for the "e-F@ctory" (its factory automation trademark). As MELCO shifts from making hardware to becoming the provider of advanced data solutions for the edge, the emerging business model foresees an increasing portion of revenue from servitization and connectivity services. In January 2021, MELCO's CEO laid out a future vision in which his company is no longer an electronics company at all, but a software solutions provider.[43]

These transitions and advances are managed with a mix of old and new approaches to human resource management. In line with lifetime employment tradition, MELCO is morphing into a software solutions provider without massive layoffs. In R&D, the knowledge of existing engineers is being transferred and expanded to contribute to MELCO's in-house research in AI/ML. For instance, when MELCO exited the cell phone business, the cipher algorithm specialists were kept on board and retrained to specialize on encryption technologies for the edge. At the same time, other hallmarks of lifetime employment such as seniority pay were adjusted, and inventors are now rewarded with high bonuses.

---

scandal was expected to only accelerate MELCO's exit of hardware businesses, to become an edge computing leader.

42 Author interviews with MELCO managers and engineers, Tokyo, October 2018 and July 2019. Data sourced from www.mitsubishielectric.com/en/about/corporate_data/index.page

43 "Mitsubishi Denki, Sugiyama shachō 'Mō haado ni shigamitsukanai'" (MELCO CEO Sugiyama says company no longer clinging to its hardware businesses), *Nikkei Business*, January 29, 2021; and www.mitsubishielectric.com/fa/sols/efactory/index.html

In this competition at the technology frontier, MELCO's R&D efforts are mostly self-funded and not typically shared with domestic competitors, as was common during the industrial policies of the old style. Unlike in the post-WWII period, when cash-strapped and technology-hungry companies joined government-organized R&D consortia, MELCO possesses most of the resources it needs and the in-house intellectual property to expand. It will form competitive alliances and engage in open innovation only where that creates synergies. Bureaucrats have little guidance to offer at the technology frontier, and MELCO's main competitors include domestic companies, while strategic allies may be abroad. The best way for the government to support the global, high-risk, deep-tech technology bets of Japanese companies is to create an enabling environment, such as through funding incentives for R&D or creating extra demand for emerging technologies through infrastructure investments.

4.4 Global Production Networks and the Relevance of Manufacturing

Since the 1970s, Japan's largest companies have built vast global financial and production networks. The post-WWII global expansion began in the 1960s, but what truly fueled their foreign direct investment (FDI) was the call for "voluntary export restraints" by the US government beginning in the 1970s. These were ramped up during the US–Japan trade war beginning in the 1980s and led to a fear of "hollowing out" (*kūdōka*) of Japan's domestic manufacturing base. Indeed, the percentage of the domestic workforce in manufacturing fell from a height of 28.6 percent in 1972 to 16.5 percent in 2019 (Figure 7, top line). This led to fears that Japanese manufacturing was in terminal decline.[44]

However, two other important developments occurred during this period that underscore the continued relevance of manufacturing for Japan's economy. The first is the increase in the contribution of exports to total GDP, from 8.8 percent in 1995, with the onset of the post-bubble crisis, to 18 percent recently (lower line). This suggests an increase in productivity and value added in manufacturing, as fewer workers contribute more. These data validate Schaede's (2020) concept of the "aggregate niche strategy," which refers to the repositioning of Japanese companies, away from low-margin consumer end products to being the technology anchor of Asian supply chains in much higher-margin upstream input materials and components. This upgrading has increased the value capture from exports.

---

[44] Conversation at a Japan conference at the University of Michigan, November 2019. This thinking reflects reporting on Japanese industry in various media; e.g., "Decline in manufacturing," *The Japan Times*, February 25, 2013.

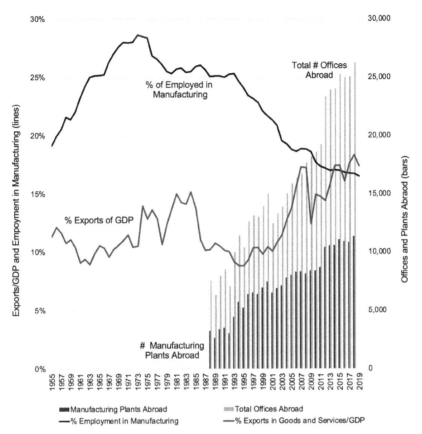

Figure 7 Employment in manufacturing, export contribution to GDP, and number of offices and production plants abroad, 1955–2019

Source: Calculated and constructed from Japan government, *2019 nendo kokumin keizai tōsan* and *Kaigai jigyō katsudō chōsa*; FRED economic data

Also occurring during this period was a steady rise in FDI and production abroad. The bars in Figure 7 show the growth in the number of manufacturing-related business and production sites since 1988, when these survey data were first collected. Today, Japan's manufacturing industry reports over 26,000 global production plants and offices. When nonmanufacturing sectors, sales offices, and R&D centers are included, a 2019 METI survey of almost 30,000 Japanese firms reported more than 74,000 Japanese locations abroad.[45]

In monetary terms, between 1996 and 2019, Japanese private sector FDI amounted to $3.6 trillion in foreign assets. In 2019 alone, Japanese companies

---

[45] METI Press Release, "Results of the 49th Basic Survey on Overseas Business Activities (July 2019 Survey) Compiled", May 27, 2020, www.meti.go.jp/english/press/2020/0527_003 .html

invested more than $310 billion abroad, including a large number of foreign acquisitions and sizable investments in Southeast Asian banking and manufacturing.[46] Looking at manufacturing only, over the past decade foreign sales generated through foreign operations have amounted to about 50 percent of total Japanese manufacturing sales and ordinary income, and 35 percent of total sales for all industries. For the year 2019, the METI survey reported roughly $88 billion investments in foreign plant and equipment (not counting M&A), total foreign sales of about $3 trillion, and profits of $137 billion.[47] These foreign sales are not included in Japan's GDP, which was about $5.3 trillion in 2019, leading to a significant underreporting of Japan's global economic activity.

Japan's government is proactively supporting these global production networks by forging trade agreements to ensure Japanese property rights abroad and reduce trade barriers of all sorts. Thus, the focus of industrial policy is turning away from domestic industry-based coordination, and to global trade policies in the form of geo-economic strategies to ease global market access and protect foreign assets (Katada 2020). But unlike the industrial policies of old, the government cannot coordinate global business operations in the same way as domestic ones. Future policies will have to be about creating and shaping the environment where companies compete.

5 The DX and People: New Employment Patterns and Reskilling

The combination of the DX and demographic change is bringing new requirements for worker specialization, retraining, and mobility in the shrinking workforce. At the *gemba* level – whether it is the shopfloor, the vertical farm, the distribution center, or the construction site – the DX means less demand for humans who do repetitive jobs, and greater need for specialists who can steer and control the digital processes. For the highly educated, the labor shortage brings a tremendous increase in bargaining power, just at a time when society is demanding more work–life balance and individual career choices. And even though it will take several years before processes ranging from garbage collection to logistics and home construction will be fully automized, companies have already begun to adjust core features of the lifetime employment system. Novel in-house corporate training, reskilling, and rotation patterns are being developed to create pathways for talent, supported by "job-based" rather than generalist hiring patterns. While a gradual progress of labor reforms has brought

---

[46] METI, 2019 business activity survey in Japan (2019nen kigyō katsudō kihon chōsa kakuhō), version June 29, 2020, www.meti.go.jp/statistics/tyo/kikatu/result-2/2019kakuho.html, and www.jetro.go.jp/en/reports/statistics.html

[47] METI, "49th foreign business activity survey," cited earlier.

many real adjustments over the previous two decades, in the 2020s the DX, in combination with the COVID-19 pandemic, combined to challenge the previous trade-offs and accepted patterns of Japan's traditional employment system.

5.1 The Redesign of Lifetime Employment

As we saw in Section 3, the backbone of Japan's postwar political economy was a social contract anchored on lifetime employment. This worked well in a fast-growing economy. However, increasing rigidities over time combined with slower growth to amplify the downsides of this system, including the cost of hiring mistakes, inert hierarchies, and slack.

From the company perspective, lifetime employment brings significant benefits (Pfeffer and Baron 1988; Schaede 2008). Job security translates into loyalty and dedication, as employees identify with the company, embrace teamwork and comradery, and promote knowledge sharing. Due to wage parity and perceived equality, morale is typically high. Companies invest in employee skill formation and reap the benefits of highly company-specific knowledge and organizational learning. Not worried about being replaced or having their salaries cut, employees are happy to accept new assignments and train younger colleagues, thus ensuring the accumulation of tacit knowledge across the entire organization, as well as control over intellectual property. It is also easier to groom leadership candidates.

On the flip side, lifetime employment is also expensive, because it makes labor a fixed cost. Because over 60 percent of Japanese employees work in rigid career paths with lockstep promotions, integration of mid-career hires into the corporate hierarchy is difficult. The limited market for mid-career job-changers inhibits the exchange of ideas and reinforces rigid work processes. So-called hiring mistakes, who are not a good fit with the organization, find themselves sidelined in unproductive assignments, while lockstep promotion may cause complacency and loss of morale. Structurally, a company's workforce becomes top-heavy over time, and benefits and pension costs rise.

By the early 2000s, the costs of lifetime employment began to outweigh the benefits, and the system began to crack. Its slow decline was precipitated by the "ice-age" hiring stop during the 1990s recession following the collapse of the bubble economy. Given rigid patterns of lockstep promotion and cumulative corporate training, college graduates in the late 1990s and early 2000s fell out of the regular workforce altogether and became known as the "lost generation." Companies, for their part, missed out on young talent and turned to hiring more nonregular workers on limited contracts. Since the early 2000s, these contract workers also included a small yet fast-growing cadre of highly skilled specialists, such as in IT. Multiple forms of employment began to emerge, the job market became more liquid, and mid-career job-changing more frequent. Societal assumptions of a "good career" slowly adjusted.

By 2020, job mobility had increased sharply, including among those in lifetime positions, such that the idea of what it means to be a lifetime employee and the expectations around the associated reciprocal obligations have now shifted. In 2020, the time-honored spring hiring round (*shūkatsu*) that meant hiring occurred only once a year, began to be phased out (Schaede 2020). Its kiss of death was a growing trend, beginning in the late 2010s, for recent hires to immediately look for another job. A 2019 survey of 1,260 recent company hires revealed that 57 percent were open to a job change, and the portion of new hires that immediately reentered the job search had increased by 30 percent between 2017 and 2019.[48] In terms of job-changing within ten years of the first employment, a 2018 survey showed that 19 percent of respondents in their twenties and thirties had already changed their jobs. The main motivations were to find a job with a better work–life balance (60 percent of respondents) and to earn a higher salary (40 percent). Overall, 72 percent of Japanese millennials thought that job-changing was a positive, forward-looking thing to do.[49]

As this growing mobility opens fresh prospects and increases the bargaining power of the top talent, it undermines the internal logic of the entire system. Recall that lifetime employment can only work if both sides remain fully committed to the quid pro quo whereby employers offer job security, training, and pensions, in return for the employee's surrender of choice in career path, location, and even working hours. The company must have this flexibility to assign employees as needed to be able to commit to keeping all employed. At the height of this "membership system" in the late twentieth century, employees self-identified not in terms of their job or personal expertise, but their company. Employees who left their company mid-career (called *datsu-sara*, "leaving the salaryman existence behind") were seen as traitors and had their membership revoked.

However, as the top talent is now becoming more inclined to change employers mid-career, even as labor scarcity is increasing, the balance between both

---

[48] "Tenshoku, kahan ga teikō nashi" (Majority not opposed to job-changing), *Nikkei Shinbun*, May 27, 2019; "Nyūshago sugu 'sai-shūkatsu' kyūzō: jōken awazu, kizoku ishiki mo usuku" (Rapid increase in "second shūkatsu" immediately after the job start: Conditions are not met and sense of belonging is weak), *Nikkei Shinbun*, August 7, 2018. This is true even in agriculture; "Shinsotsu tenshokusha ga nōgyō bunya de kyūkakudaichū" (New graduates and job changers on the rise in agriculture), *Smart Agri*, April 26, 2018, https://smartagri-jp.com/farmer/24

[49] "Mainabi chōsa, tenshokuritsu 5% no jōshō: 20dai no sonzaikan takamaru" (Mainabi survey: Job-changing rate has topped 5 percent, the presence of millennials is becoming more important), *Nikkei Shinbun*, April 23, 2019.

sides' rights and responsibilities has become unstable. For employees, successful job-hopping requires having specialized, marketable skills as opposed to corporate-specific knowledge. As such, the best and brightest are demanding fewer rotations, deeper skills, and more say in their training and focus. For companies, it no longer pays to invest so heavily in employees if they may carry the fruits of that investment elsewhere. And because the most talented employees are most likely to change jobs, employers must be concerned about an emerging hybrid system where talented employees can change jobs easily, but job security is still expected by all others. Companies could lose their best talent while being stuck with those unable to find another position. The 2020–2021 pandemic further amplified this bifurcation between the demands of the highly mobile, most skilled employees, and society's demand for stable employment. While the new global uncertainty raised the bargaining power of those able to perform under the difficult circumstances, it also increased the desire for job security in a large portion of the workforce.

In response to this bifurcation, companies have begun to design more flexible processes to accommodate the top tier while modifying workplace expectations overall. Since the early 2000s, more and more companies have introduced a meritocracy pay and promotion system that exempted the top talent from lockstep advancements. Early adopters included Orix, Recruit, Rakuten, Softbank, Takeda, and Nidec, as well as many professional services such as consulting. Their HR reforms paved the way toward developing a new logic of hiring that emphasizes individual skills in certain job categories. In the 2020s, the traditional "membership" employment system was challenged by a newly emerging "job-based system" whereby a company first identifies its specific needs at a given time, and then hires specifically to fill those openings.[50] Moreover, the phaseout of the annual, highly choreographed *shūkatsu* hiring rounds, beginning in 2019, has allowed hiring at different times of the year, as well as at mid-career levels. Together, all these have combined to facilitate job-changing by highly competent employees and shift to a needs-based approach to hiring as companies search for talent. Work content and work patterns are evolving accordingly.

All this is causing ruptures in the existing system. For companies, pension reform is imminent, as the increase in labor mobility requires a new system of pension transferability. For employees, within-company competition and performance transparency runs counter to traditional business norms of saving face and preserving the appearance of egalitarianism. Yet, the shift to meritocracy

---

[50] The "job-based model" (*jobu-gata koyō*) was first discussed in the Employment Working Group (*Koyō waaking gurūpu*) of the Regulatory Reform Council meeting in June 2013, see www8 .cao.go.jp/kisei-kaikaku/kaigi/publication/130605/item4.pdf

also enables the top talent to rise to the top faster, and companies to pivot into new growth businesses.

All these ongoing changes received a legal basis through the 2019 labor law reform, called the "Workstyle Reforms" (*Hatarakikata-kaikaku*). The new law brought a fundamental rethinking of workplace rules, which can be categorized into three broad areas: (1) pay and wages; (2) welfare, work hours, and diversity; and (3) contract flexibility and a novel "dual jobs" system that allows an employee to work for two employers simultaneously (*fukugyō-kengyō*).[51] Together, these push companies to value outcomes more than process, and specialization more than general knowledge. Even though the transition proceeds only slowly, the emerging wage system suggests a trade-off between equality (lockstep promotions and seniority pay) and equity (meritocracy), as long-term employment is pitched against individualistic career advancement. In contrast to the previous system where pay was based on tenure with the company, wages are increasingly determined based on performance and contribution, and are beginning to differ by job category.

A large portion of the 2019 Workstyle Reforms is the new emphasis on work–life balance, and a stronger role for employees in making individual career choices. New rules on working hours, overtime, vacation time, and paid leave for family reasons have been introduced, and violations are now punished. Various surveys of large Japanese companies on their goals for implementing workstyle reforms confirm that change is real. Figure 8 shows the results of a 2020 survey, on the corporate goals with implementing workstyle reform, in a comparison with results for 2017. For 2020, the top goals were employee retention, workforce diversity and inclusion, attracting better talent, and compliance with the 2019 labor law. In contrast, the broader targets of innovation and globalization received fewer mentions than before. When asked what measures they took in pursuit of retention, diversity, and attractiveness, 95 percent of companies listed "reduction of working hours by limiting overtime" and "encouraging vacations," which are both now legal requirements. Almost two-thirds of companies revised daily work routine rules, and 57 percent created a shared, or "free address," office design and facilitated working from home (Deloitte Tohmatsu Consulting 2020). These reforms were greatly accelerated by the 2020 COVID-19 pandemic, which brought even more flexible work regimes.

Still, with all these modifications, there remains a sizable portion of Japanese society that considers offering lifetime employment as the most important social responsibility of the large corporation. Companies, too, are keen to

---

[51] See www.mhlw.go.jp/hatarakikata/index.html and JIL (2018), Vogel (2018), Schaede (2020).

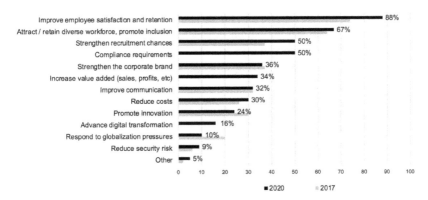

Figure 8 Corporate goals with the implementation of workstyle reforms
Source: Constructed from Deloitte Tohmatsu Consulting (2020)

uphold the many advantages of stable employment, especially with the shrinking workforce. These countervailing trends dampen the speed of change and incentivize companies to invest in retraining existing workers instead of replacing them (see next). But at the margin, and among Japan's top performing companies, the 2019 reforms are a watershed event, as they rewrite the quid pro quo between the top talent over their employers and lubricate the entire system.

5.2 The "Dual Jobs" System

The irony of Japan's looming labor shortage is that companies are eager to lock in young, talented employees with lifetime employment contracts, just at a time when the young talent is interested in exploring more individualized careers. To square this circle, the 2019 Workstyle Reforms include a section that allows companies to introduce a system of "dual jobs" (*fukugyō-kengyō*) if they so desire. There is some ambiguity regarding terminology, but an important difference is made between *kengyō* (concurrent employment) and *fukugyō* (side job). In a side job, a worker in a nondemanding job takes on a gig assignment in their spare time. This gig economy work increased greatly during the 2020 pandemic year, when many people who found themselves working fewer hours, from home, used the opportunity to supplement their income.[52]

Of special interest here is the concurrent employment, or what Schaede (2021) has labeled the "career-track dual job" (*sōgōshoku kengyō*). This system is highly unusual in international comparison. In most countries, including the

---

[52] "Hatarakikata, gigu, terewaaku no saki: miete-kita seichō to hizumi" (The future of workstyles, gig, and telework: What we've learned about growth and distortions), *Nikkei*, June 28, 2021; "Gigu-waakaa, manzokudo takaku" (Gig workers have high job satisfaction rates), *Nikkei*, January 12, 2021.

United States, full-time employees in professional tracks are not allowed to also work elsewhere, and this limitation is usually stipulated in the employment contract. Working for two employers is seen as problematic in terms of employee loyalty, conflicts of interest, competitive trade secrets, and intellectual property protection.

In Japan, the rules governing terms of employment are laid out in each company's own "business rules" (*shūgyō kisoku),* which form the basis of employment and spell out the rules and regulations of the company, including wages, working hours, vocational training, retirement pay, as well as specific codes of behavior and even the dress code. To help especially smaller firms draft this document, the government issues an annual template. Beginning with the 2018 template, the government removed a provision that employees could not hold a second job concurrently, leaving it to each company to allow or prohibit their employees to serve two masters. In 2019, this change was adopted in the Workstyle Reforms labor law.

It is important to realize that the dual job system is not expected to grow into large numbers. Rather, the purpose is to allow companies to attract, train, and promote top-tier talent on the fast track, all without toppling the tenure-based, lockstep hierarchy that still exists for rank-and-file employees. Thus, the "dual jobs" option creates a welcome pathway for the highest performers. In terms of the DX, large companies can use the growing labor mobility to their advantage, by granting their best talent a type of "innovation sabbatical" during which they can acquire additional skills in AI/ML, data mining, edge computing, or robotics, as well as the entrepreneurial spirit to develop new business segments for the large company (METI 2019b, 2020b).

Even though administrative complications loom large, by 2021 about half of Japan's largest employers had removed the exclusivity clause from their business rules.[53] For many, the goal is not only to satisfy the top performers, but also to place low-cost bets on DX technologies and associated skill formation. Some companies allow employees to go on leave for work at a startup company, for a while or on certain days of the week. If successful, the original employer stands to benefit as an early investor in the technology; if unsuccessful, they will gladly take the employee back, filled with new experience and impressions. For example, at Panasonic, ten employees went on this track in the first two years of the program. Similarly, chip maker Murata allowed several employees to join

---

[53] Interviews with business and government, Tokyo, 2018 and 2019; "Fukugyō kaikin, shuyō kigyō no 5-wari" (50 percent of largest firmest allow dual jobs), *Nikkei Shinbun,* May 20, 2019; "Fukugyō mitomeru kigyō, Kyūshū – Okinawa de yonwari chikaku, Teikoku Data" (TDB reports about 40 percent of companies in Kyushu and Okinawa allow side jobs), *Nikkei Shinbun,* March 24, 2021.

a startup that works on AI-powered communication robots, while NTT and Osaka Gas created similar sabbatical systems.[54]

A variant of this system is the sharp rise in independent contractors (*kojin jigyō-nushi*), that is, highly skilled specialists, hired by large companies on very high-paid, short-term contracts to work on one project, such as in IT solutions, specialized engineering, or business consulting. They enter the statistics as "nonregular" workers, but they are not at all marginal parts of the work force. Rather, they offer highly specialized skills that afford companies access to advanced DX specialization on a contract basis, without destroying the existing wage parity for the main corps of regular employees. The successes of these contractors have brought further fluidity into the workforce, as other high performers follow their paths. Some companies are shifting to relying on contractors for an increasing fraction of their entire workforce, thereby introducing cutting-edge, deep-tech knowledge to the company.[55]

5.3 Case Study: Recruit Holdings Co., Ltd.

A leading example of these novel work patterns comes from Recruit, a personnel and appointment booking agency. Recruit engages in organizing job fairs, job- and headhunting, and temporary staffing, as well as automatic reservations and payment systems. Its vast network and deep reach in personal data collection and data mining have made Recruit Japan's most advanced player in the GAFA (Google, Amazon, Facebook, Apple) league (Buche et al. 2016; Schaede 2020). Recruit operates globally, including through acquisitions of US human resource companies Indeed (2012) and Glassdoor (2018), which made it the world's largest online staffing agency in 2021.

Within Japan, Recruit dominates not only as a staffing agency, but also as a total data services provider for small firms such as restaurants, hairdressers, and shopkeepers. For businesses, services include wireless reservation and payment systems, and finance and bookkeeping. For consumers, Recruit offers not only employment services but also personal matchmaking and lifestyle arrangements, from apartment rentals to wedding planning. As a result, Recruit has access to detailed information on daily-life behavior, work and living situation, finances and, perhaps most importantly, behavioral changes of a large portion of Japan's population. These data allow Recruit to forecast work

---

[54] "Sutaato-appu de 'musha shugyō', Murata Seisakusho nado dōnyū" (Murata and others introduce "warrior training" at startup companies), *Nikkei Shinbun*, November 5, 2020.

[55] See, for example, "Shain no yaku 1-wari ga kojin jigyō-nushi ni! Tanita no, kigyōto kojinka 'hikitsukeau' kankeisei no tsukurikata" (About 10 percent of employees as contractors! How Tanita is creating a new "attraction model" for companies and individuals), August 4, 2020, https://seleck.cc/1419

and life satisfaction, likelihood of job-changing, and much more. In 2020, Recruit Holdings had 50,000 employees working in its main business and 366 subsidiaries and affiliates in 60 countries, generating total global revenues of roughly \$25 billion. And, the company claims to generate roughly 1,000 new business ideas annually and promises rapid growth in DX business segments.[56]

Recruit is also a trailblazer with its own employment processes. The company pays high wages based only on meritocracy. After a few years with the company, employees are fully expected and encouraged to change jobs or start their own company, and this is built into the pay and incentive structure. Unlike the common practice of treating job-changers as traitors, those who move on continue to be part of the larger Recruit family, and former employees may even return.[57] This freedom and the opportunities created through the Recruit network, paired with the assurance of belonging, attract Japan's very best college graduates in AI, big data, and other specialized DX knowledge to work at Recruit for a few years before launching their own business in the digital economy.

Other companies have designed similar systems. DeNA, the mobile portal and e-commerce company, also maintains a "hub" system (Namba 2013). In the mid-2010s, Sony and All Nippon Airlines (ANA) started programs that funded young engineers who started their own company, with the first right of refusal to acquire the eventual product. Employees also have the option to return if their startup fails.

Thus, rising labor mobility and the dual jobs system allow established companies to structure transitions in and out of a lifetime employment job while preserving employee loyalty and dedication. Even if the total numbers may remain small, the dual job system still opens fresh avenues for companies to create and maintain processes for open innovation. This enables them to better compete in the DX without fully abandoning the aspects of the old system that remain desirable.

5.4 Reskilling and Education Reform

Japan's looming labor shortage is playing out before the background of a historically low unemployment rate in Japan. Between 1989 and 2019, the highest unemployment rate recorded was 5.5 percent in 2009, after the global financial crisis. Despite the COVID-19 pandemic, in 2020 it remained below 3 percent (OECD 2021). The tightness in the labor market, coupled with the

---

[56] Recruit Annual Report 2020, see https://recruit-holdings.com/who/reports/2020/pdf/insideout 2020_en.pdf

[57] Recruit maintains a website of alumni with current startup information; https://matome.naver.jp /odai/2134855976914479801

ageing workforce, has two important implications for the DX and Japan's future competitiveness. On the one hand, it reduces concerns about worker replacement through automation. From manufacturing to cashier- and other self-services, Japanese are comparatively more inclined to embrace technology advances because these do not threaten their livelihood. On the other hand, it necessitates the retraining of people to fulfil new roles. Immigration policies have recently been revised to facilitate the hiring of foreigners with specialized skills, but implementation remains slow and deliberate. This means the inflow of foreign talent will continue to be incremental. As companies cannot hire outside talent, they must compete in the DX with the employees they have. They have no choice but to develop new ways to retain and retrain their workforce.

In this transition of employees to new assignments, long-standing patterns of Japan's political economy are proving helpful. As the DX is arriving alongside a labor shortage, job stability and retraining, which have long been seen as socially desirable, are also cost-rational for companies. Employers can and must continue their role in providing training, just in a different way with altered content. And, employees are likely to accept reskilling assignments, thanks to the traditional lifetime relationship between employers and employees, which reduces fears of displacement and has long included training on the job.

By 2022, many of Japan's largest companies had launched large-scale retraining programs, in combination with designing specialized DX career tracks. These "reskilling" (*manabi-naoshi*) programs aim to make white collar and factory workers DX-fluent (IPA 2020). For example, in 2021, Canon launched a six-months "AI and cloud" program for 1,500 employees, consisting of classes in programming, cybersecurity, quantitative methods, and general "digital knowledge." Instructors are recruited among in-house engineers and IT specialists as well as outside contractors, such as Microsoft. In 2020, Furukawa Electric, founded in 1884 as an infrastructure electric components manufacturer, announced a pivot toward an "industry 4.0" factory automation supplier by 2030. The requisite training of employees was to be accomplished through the 2021 acquisition of "AI-demy," a company with a learning platform for advanced technologies and AI. With this academy, Furukawa began to build out an additional core competence in "DX human resource creation," to be sold as a service to other companies. Meanwhile, the large financial group SMBC sent 50,000 employers to an e-learning class on digital finance and fintech, while Hitachi dispatched 16,000 employees to digital education. At beverage company Suntory, 3,900 handpicked employees older than forty years were sent off to a DX training course. These are just a few examples of the emerging trends of reskilling associated with changing corporate strategies for the DX competition.[58]

The government, too, has identified the upgrading of human resource (HR) management as an additional means to raise competitiveness in the DX. A 2021 "Ito Report on DX HR" (METI 2020c) proposes a more salient role for HR in corporate strategy. Under lifetime employment and regular on-the-job rotation, the HR department was usually seen as necessary and powerful, yet at its core HR was an administrative support function, like IT. Various METI study groups have suggested that the DX is now making the quality of a company's human capital a key competitive resource, and thus the HR function a strategic asset. Thus, large firms are advised to create an additional position in the C-Suite, namely: that of the chief human resources officer (CHRO) (METI 2019b, 2020b).

At the same time, the government is also looking at educational reforms, to prepare the next generation of DX workers through a revision of the high school curriculum. Although Japan's education system is sometimes denigrated as rigid and too focused on rote learning, Japanese students fare well in international comparison. In the 2018 PISA ranking of international student assessments, Japan's fifteen-year-olds ranked first in math and second in science; in total world rankings that include China, Japanese students still ranked in the top ten.[59] This was unchanged over 2015 and 2012, to show that in basic education Japan consistently outperforms Western nations. Moreover, the high school completion rate in Japan has long been 99 percent, meaning that almost all Japanese enjoy at least twelve years of schooling (MEXT 2020).

But how to train these students for the DX is now the challenge for MEXT, the Ministry of Education, Culture, Sports, Science and Technology, which launched an encompassing curriculum reform in 2020 (Cabinet Office 2019; MEXT 2020). MEXT is often viewed as resistant to change, but in this case there was no choice as this DX pivot was directly ordered by the Cabinet Office (see Section 6). Even though MEXT took a while to develop the new programs, once determined, Japan's centralized education system allowed a comparatively swift rollout of "active learning" and IT instruction initiatives. IT classes are now mandatory at all Japanese high schools, and many are offering introductory classes to AI. There is

---

[58] "Canon, kōjōjūgyōin ni DX kyōiku: seichō shokushu e haichi tankan" (At Canon, DX education for all workers: job transfer into growth businesses), *Nikkei*, July 7, 2021; "Furukawa Denkō to Aidemii, shihon gyōmu teikyō teiketsu: DX jinzai kyōiku kara shinki jigyō kaihatsu made kyōdō de jitsugen" (Furukawa electric and Aidemii form capital and business alliance: jointly realizing DX human resource development and new business development), June 22, 2021, www.furukawa.co.jp/release/2021/kei_20210622.html

[59] OECD Programme for International Student Assessment (PISA) 2018 results, www.oecd.org/pisa/publications/pisa-2018-results.htm. See also MEXT, "PISA 2019 no pointo," December 3, 2019, www.nier.go.jp/kokusai/pisa/pdf/2018/01_point.pdf

also a curriculum initiative for more STEM education. This began in 2020 with a "one PC for each student" initiative, as "learning from home" under the COVID-19 pandemic made it painfully clear that Japan is lagging in this category. At the university level, too, AI literacy is scheduled to be included in sciences and liberal arts tracks. The shrinking society is increasing competition for students even among the country's best universities, which has led to fresh curriculum design and course offerings in data science, mathematics, and AI-related tools. The government has also launched a massive open online course as part of its 2019 AI Strategy (Cabinet Office 2019; MEXT 2020).

In AI-related research spending, Japan also compares favorably in international comparison. In 2020, the venture capital firm Thundermark Capital produced a global "AI research ranking," based on private and public research dollars spent on AI-related research. The study found that the United States topped all others with $1.6 trillion, followed by Europe (counted as one, with $500 billion), China ($280 billion), Canada ($155 billion), South Korea ($77 billion), Japan, and Israel (both at roughly $58 billion).[60] Not assessed were the significant investments by Asian companies, especially from Korea and Japan, in US-based research in AI, such as through venture capital investments in Silicon Valley and elsewhere. In the 2020s, it was estimated that more than 1,000 Japanese companies operated so-called open innovation research and investment centers in Silicon Valley, many of which were also learning centers for corporate employees.[61] In addition to showing the great corporate commitments to DX innovation, these global innovation investments also remind us that putting borders around AI innovation does not make a lot of sense, given the borderless reach of the DX and the speed of innovation dissemination and adoption.

Thus, through a combination of corporate efforts at reskilling, organizational renewal, labor reform, high school and university curriculum reforms, and massive investments in innovation, in the early 2020s, Japan is preparing its workforce to compete in new businesses and technologies at the digital frontier. For the political economy, this means balancing what still works while dropping what does not, all the while maintaining a system that is stable and at its core remains mostly egalitarian.

6 The DX and the State: Toward a New Political Economy

This section lays out the evolution of the role of the state in Japan's political economy as of 2022. As the two disruptions coincide for Japan, the government

---

[60] "2020nen no AI kenkyū rankingu," *AI NOW*, February 25, 2021, https://ainow.ai/2021/02/25/252580/

[61] Author interviews, Silicon Valley, 2019-2020.

is increasingly salient in shaping an environment in which companies can compete globally, and in redesigning domestic institutions so that the country can grab hold of the "lucky moment." One challenge is how to assess progress, because the institutions of industrial policy as we knew them in the twentieth century, and common metrics such as employment by industry or sector, are also being disrupted by the DX. Since the 1990s, the tools that bureaucrats used to guide companies have been slowly but systematically removed. As of 2022, the transformation of Japan's political economy was in full swing: ministries were moving from industry-based to sector-based policymaking, and the relationship between politicians and bureaucrats had changed. The labor shortage combined with the decline in the power of the ministries to cause a "Kasumigaseki crisis," expressed most visibly in a drastic decline in applications by the country's best and brightest to join the civil service. A call for "architectural change" (METI 2017; Nishiyama 2021) to break down ministerial silos and unify policymaking was heeded in 2021 when the prime minister charged the newly appointed "Minister of the DX" to create a "Digital Agency" that would cut across all ministries as if it were the platform anchoring different verticals, which should no longer be thought of as ministries, but as economic activities. While it remains unclear whether these reforms will be successful, as of 2022, all signs were pointing to an overhaul of the core features of Japan's political economy.

6.1 From Industrial Policy to Industry Structure Policy

The DX is bringing a shift in the balance of power, resource dependencies, and perceptions of utility among companies, people, and the state. This requires new forms of governance. Some of these shifts are continuations of changes that began in the 1990s, and the trajectory has been chronicled in the literature. For example, Pempel's (1998) "Regime Shift" was an early analysis of the political system reforms and adjustments of power relations between elite bureaucrats and politicians. Amyx and Drysdale (2003) analyzed institutional reforms, and Vogel (2006) showed how industry interests and government coordination were remodeled. Schaede (2008) labeled the business implications of these system changes a "strategic inflection point."

The DX now means that companies are competing in the global race to the DX technology frontier not as industry-based teams but as individual athletes. State-led coaching and coordination of domestic industries are no longer impactful, or even possible. Unlike the rapid growth period of catching up, the future is uncertain, and the state's task is to enable individual companies to compete as best as they can in an unknown arena against existing and future global competitors. Thus, even as the state is addressing ongoing challenges of stagnation and a lower economic growth trajectory, it also must design new ways to support future growth chances.

A second challenge for the government is that companies are straddling not only industries but also economies and sectors. They no longer fall neatly into categories such as manufacturing, or certain industries. Since the 1990s, ministries have responded to this blurring of boundaries by competing for jurisdiction, and by the early 2000s this had resulted in infighting and rampant program duplication. For example, in 2017, nine different ministries and agencies had established fourteen mostly government-funded investment funds that offered competing programs of several billions each, to fund startup activities, regional revitalization, and infrastructure and energy innovation.[62] By 2020, the intragovernment competition had reached a point where a reorganization of government itself became urgent.

Meanwhile, METI has shifted from industrial *sector* to industry *structure* policies (Kohno 2002; METI 2017; RIETI 2020). METI's 2001 reorganization was a first acknowledgement that the previous patterns of industrial policy implementation based on tight, domestic networks, and constant negotiations with companies were no longer effective. Policymaking was pushed beyond the former areas of trade and commerce, and into broader areas of economic policy and adjacent areas, such as science and technology, health and labor, construction, and even justice. While the specificity of industrial policy declined, its realm has broadened, from climate change, recycling and ESG investment, infrastructure investments for the DX (e.g., ubiquitous connectivity), measures to ease the conduct of business (e.g., deregulation of permits and licenses), and subsidies promoting the use of technologies such as AI and IoT.

To be sure, some of the old patterns of ministerial coordination continue to exist, especially in highly regulated industries such as energy and telecommunications. For example, the 2011 Fukushima nuclear disaster highlighted continuing deep ties between METI and the power companies. A 2021 scandal involving a telecommunications company also involved the prime minister's son, underscoring that old networks and patterns of interaction continue in places. Yet, with the differentiated evolution of industries and sectors, what used to be fairly uniform story of government guidance has variegated further with ministries exercising different levels of influence over their respective industries.

---

[62] "14 fando mo ranritsu, yosan shōka ga yūsen" (Numbering 14, fund creation has gone haywire), *Nikkei*, August 6, 2018.

One indicator of the reduction in industry-specific guidance is that the government no longer produces five-year plans, and the Economic Planning Agency no longer exists. Indicative planning made sense when Japan was pursuing a clear goal after WWII, but since arriving on the technology frontier, such visions would border on futurology. Instead, most ministries now publish copious deliberation council reports, some exceeding several hundred pages.[63] As for METI, even though bureaucrats remain convinced that transforming industry structure and strengthening economic resilience remains an important task in a few basic infrastructure industries, the overall focus has broadened. To wit, METI's 2021 "economic and industrial policy vision" outlines six over-arching policy areas, none of which is an industry per se: the DX, environment, health, small firms and regions, resilience, and innovation reskilling (METI 2020a). Although these are all important and will affect many business outcomes, they are of a different ilk than the industry-level guidance and direction-setting of the twentieth century.

6.2 Changes in Government–Business Relations

The decline of the relative power of the bureaucracy over industry began after the burst of the bubble economy in the 1990s, when various scandals shed light on the negative aspects of post-WWII industrial policy. While real estate machinations and stock picks truncated the career of many a politician, the bureaucrats did not keep their hands entirely clean either. In 1994, opposition leader Ozawa Ichirō (1994) published a "Blueprint for a New Japan" that called for a shift in procedures for more transparency, just as the bureaucracy came under attack for its failures during the bubble economy and subsequent economic collapse. Some ministries were merged or renamed, while others had parts of their regulatory mandates removed. This was particularly true for the Ministry of Finance, which in 1998 saw the regulatory oversight over the financial industry transferred to a new FSA. This was also the final step in removing the levers of postwar financial regulation for fostering fast economic growth (Nakano 1998; Amyx 2004; Toya and Amyx 2006; Himino 2021).

The main coordination mechanisms of industrial policy – the trade associations, administrative guidance, and constant personal communication – have all changed (Amyx and Drysdale 2003). The 1994 Administrative Procedure Act (*Gyōsei tetsuzuki-hō*) aimed to make situational regulation and administrative guidance more transparent and consistent, by requiring a legal basis and a written justification signed by the cognizant bureaucrat. In some ways, this

---

[63] For example, for METI policy reports see www.meti.go.jp/shingikai/index_report.html

law only addressed procedures that the ministries had already revised. In contrast, the 2000 revision of the "National Ethics Law for Central Government Public Servants" (*Kokka kōmuin rinri hō*) made a big difference, as it greatly limited entertainment paid for by the regulated industries. This interrupted previous processes of policy brainstorming in private settings and efficient albeit nontransparent, behind-the-curtain problem solving. Many companies abolished the position of the ministry liaison. For the "Old Boy" system of senior retiring bureaucrats joining the private sector, the "cooling-off" period was extended to six months, and a direct move into an organization that the retiree used to regulate became rare. Overall, ministries–industry relations have become more muted and are now increasingly directed at the transfer of knowledge, rather than the practice of regulatory power (Suzuki 2006; Lebo 2018).

The role of trade associations has also been amended, partially due to significant antitrust reforms. Old-style price agreements and intra-industry coordination are no longer allowed (Schaede 2000; JFTC 2020). Japan's Fair Trade Commission (JFTC) was created under the US occupation, and for the early years of its existence was staffed with bureaucrats seconded from METI and MOF, who often made antitrust subservient to industrial policy. However, by the 1990s the JFTC had finally promoted its own hires into senior positions, which allowed the Commission to gain independence. Over time, the JFTC staff as well as antitrust enforcement increased significantly, and this undermined the self-regulatory functions of trade association in the name of fast economic growth.[64]

What is more, with increasing within-industry competition, companies in one industry no longer form stable coalitions. As they straddle industries in various directions, private sector interests evolve and align in different ways. The most complicated balancing act in the face of these tensions is that performed by Keidanren, the Japan Business Federation. As of 2021, this umbrella association represented 1,444 large member companies, and 109 nationwide industry associations.[65] While Keidanren was once seen as a bulwark of business lobbying, with the onset of deregulation and diverging paths and interests of its members, in 1995, Keidanren terminated donations to the Liberal Democratic Party, the leading pro-business party. In 2002, it merged with Nikkeiren, the largest employer association. As this Federation continued to represent mostly conversative viewpoints, it failed to represent the New Economy companies. Those New Japan senior managers and reformers joined

---

[64] JFTC Annual Reports, various issues, www.jftc.go.jp/en/about_jftc/annual_reports/index.html
[65] www.keidanren.or.jp/en/profile/pro001.html

the Keizai Dōyūkai (Japan Association of Corporate Executives) instead, which made the voice of business in policymaking even more multifaceted.

The nature of company-specific regulation is also under redesign. For example, in manufacturing there are many factory-level safety regulations, which stipulate that a person must ascertain that all workplace safety requirements are met, often while the machines are stopped. Advanced vision technologies, sensors, cameras, and computers could do many of these checks faster and better, in real time and without interrupting the production process. To facilitate this transition to a new regulation paradigm, a "sandbox" (suggestion box) system was introduced to invite business requests for reviews of leftover regulations.[66] In other words, as digital manufacturing arrives, METI is delegating the formulation of factory-level safety and technical standards to the private sector. Within METI there is substantial disagreement over how far this delegation ought to be pushed. The reformers are calling for a fundamental redesign in the logic of Japan's regulatory design, in which even greater discretion is given to companies so that they can respond more swiftly to technological disruptions. However, conservative voices in favor of a "safety first" approach and strict government oversight remain strong. A generational shift is beginning to be visible also in the new self-definition within the ministries. As of 2022, debate over the right course for industrial and industry structure policies continued (RIETI 2020; Toyama 2020; Nishiyama 2021).

6.3 A New Power Balance: Politicians and Bureaucrats

Just as the bureaucracy was losing it coordination tools for the private sector, it also experienced a slow yet steady pull of power into the hands of politicians. As early as the late 1970s, politicians began to contest budget ceilings set by the Ministry of Finance (Sato and Matsuzaki 1986). As politicians assumed a bigger say in the budget process, LDP policy specialists known as *"zoku"* asserted control in their specific areas of interest. Revisions of Japan's electoral rules in 1994, and greater competition from opposition parties with the economic stagnation after the collapse of the financial bubble, led many politicians to blame the bureaucrats for Japan's economic woes. This opened the doors to repeated attempts to wrestle further authority away from the ministries.

The administrative reforms of 1998 under Prime Minister Hashimoto Ryūtarō greatly strengthened the role of the prime minister and the Cabinet. The Prime Minister's Office was merged with the former Economic Planning Agency into the Cabinet Office. The reform nearly halved the number of cabinet-level ministries and agencies from twenty-two to thirteen, and included

---

[66] Interviews with METI officials in charge of this system, 2020–2021.

a review of regulations and subsidies to reduce bureaucratic intervention in the economy. The new Council on Economics and Fiscal Policy (CEFP) assumed some of MOF's budgetary powers and amplified the impact of private sector policy experts, who were selected by the prime minister. Prime Minister Koizumi Junichirō (in office 2001–2006) took full advantage of the Cabinet Office's newfound powers to implement a program of structural reforms, which signaled a clear break in Japan's postwar bureaucratic dominance.

The 1994 electoral reform brought significant partisan realignment and new patterns of government formation. The revised electoral rules made party identification much more important and incited more open battles over economic, political, and administrative reforms (Reed et al. 2009, Krauss and Pekkanen 2011). For Japan's political economy, the most important aspect of the electoral reform is that the new, hybrid electoral system weakened the influence of the "organized vote," that is, special interests with a status quo orientation. Rather than catering to a few, narrow special interest groups, politicians began to gather votes by appealing to a broader patch of the electorate. Moreover, both the single-member districts and those with proportional representation now encourage politicians at all levels to compete based on party policy differences. This has greatly increased the relevance of policy programs and content, which in turn empowered politicians like Koizumi Junichirō and Abe Shinzō, who were not just political power brokers but also represented a certain policy vision. These reforms combined to facilitate reform driven by politicians rather than bureaucrats.

But arguably the biggest power shift occurred when the Cabinet Office assumed responsibility over bureaucratic appointments, beginning at the highest level. The right to appoint the senior ministry officials placed some politicians above bureaucrats, and it also made the Cabinet Office mission central (Takenaka 2021). From the perspective of career bureaucrats, it brought a sea change in decision-making powers as well as career incentives. Decision-making authority is now determined by the prime minister, who handpicks the senior bureaucrats to work in the Cabinet Office, including the chief cabinet secretaries and special advisors. This group of select people decides not only policy directions but sometimes even details, all the way down to the choice of words used in ministerial reports, or which private sector members to invite to the various ministerial task forces and advisory boards (Mori 2019).

Prime Minister Abe Shinzō and his "Abenomics" reform program (2012–2020) propelled reforms and further consolidated the politicians' power (Hoshi and Lipscy 2021). Abe's successors, Suga Yoshihide in 2020 and Kishida Fumio beginning in 2021, both aimed to push the entire government to embrace the DX, and to tear down the vertical divisions and end the turf battles across

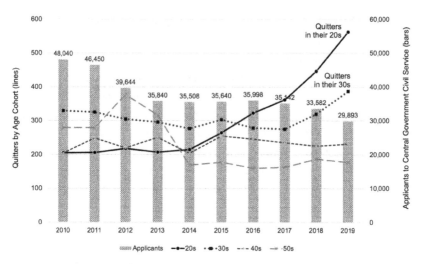

Figure 9 Voluntary resignations, by age brackets, and annual applications for national civil service exams, 2010–2020
Source: Constructed with data from Cabinet Office and National Personnel Agency[68]

and within the ministries. They envisioned a complete government reorganization, driven by the new "Minister in Charge of the Digital Transformation" in charge of a new Digital Agency, which was designed to cut across all ministries and become the catalyst for reorganization. For example, as agrotech began to turn agriculture into a de facto manufacturing industry, one suggestion was to make the Ministry of Agriculture, Fishery and Forestry just a branch of METI. While such grand-scale redrawing of responsibilities would create synergies, it was also perceived as a threat by many ministries (Cabinet Office 2020b).

6.4 The "Kasumigaseki Crisis"

The bureaucracy's decline in autonomy and power, together with the harsh working conditions of central government officials, have caused a talent drain for the central ministries. In 2020, Kōno Tarō, the then minister in charge of administrative reform, declared that Kasumigaseki – the part of Tokyo where the ministries are located – was facing a crisis.[67] Not only were fewer college graduates interested in joining the civil service, a larger portion of those who joined quit after only a few years. Figure 9 presents both trends. The vertical

---

[67] "Kasumigaseki o 'howaito-ka suru' wakate kanryō no shiki kōjō ni chūryoku, Kōno gyōkaku tantō daijin" (Administrative reform minister Kono warns that morale of young bureaucrats must be uplifted to avoid wiping out Kasumigaseki), *Yahoo News*, September 17, 2020.

[68] Sources: www.cas.go.jp/jp/gaiyou/jimu/jinjikyoku/jinji_c5.html and www.jinji.go.jp/hakusho/R1/1-3-01-data-03.html

bars show that in 2019, a total of 29,893 applicants took the national service career track exam (right axis). This marked a ten-year drop, from almost 50,000 in 2010. Of those who took the exam, barely 4 percent passed, which was half the success rate of 2003, indicating a decline in the quality of the applicant pool. A similar downward trend holds for local civil service positions, where applications have shrunk by a third, from 160,000 in 2011 to 112,000 in 2017, and the passing rate halved from about to 10 percent to 5.6 percent (Kōmuin sōken 2021).

Equally worrisome for the government was the increase in voluntary resignations from the civil services (there even is a word for it: *datsu-kan,* "leaving the bureaucrat existence behind"). Figure 9 shows this in lines by age group (left axis). The resignations are highest, and rising the fastest, among central ministry bureaucrats in their twenties. This is an elite group of young college graduates who passed a grueling entrance examination only to leave within a few years. Resignations by young bureaucrats in their thirties show a similar increase. In a 2021 survey, the main reasons for quitting were the desire to find more attractive work, have a better work–life balance, and earn a higher salary.[69]

Demographic change and the looming labor shortage will only amplify these developments. Increasing returns to specialization and the end of lockstep promotions in the private sector have significantly raised the opportunity costs for Japan's best and brightest, who can now enjoy a fast-track career path and command a much higher wage outside government. What is more, the benefits of a government job may no longer outweigh the costs, not just because of the loss of power to the bureaucrats, but also because the borderless and speedy aspects of DX make policy outcomes from ministries much less visible and tangible.

On the bright side, however, these trends are counterbalanced by the newly emerging role for the government. The DX will also create new areas where ministries matter. Just as the DX is creating business opportunities, it is also presenting fresh areas for bureaucrats to offer guidance and shape policy. For example, the DX will require not only more cybersecurity but also intellectual property protection. These needs have greatly elevated the roles of the National Police Agency and Japan Patent Office. Trade policy,

---

[69] "Kyaria kanryō shigansha 14.5% gen, kako saidai, hatarakikata eikyō" (Career bureaucrat applications down 14.5 percent highest decline on record, attributed to work style), *Nikkei Shinbun,* April 16, 2021. "Kōno-daijin ni kiita: 'Karōshi-rain' no chōkikan-zangyō ga ōkō suru Kasumigaseki, hataraki-kaikaku ha hontōni jitsugen dekiru no ka?" (We asked Minister Kono: With rampant overtime work, is workstyle reform possible?), *Business Insider,* January 13, 2021; website of Kōno Tarō, "Kiki ni chokumen suru Kasumigaski" (Kasumigaseki facing crisis). November 18, 2020, www.taro.org/2020/11/危機に直面する霞ヶ関.php

too, is becoming much more important. In addition to negotiating a myriad of bi- and multilateral trade agreements, the government also needs to protect Japan's sizable and growing stock of foreign direct investment (as seen in Section 4.4). In 2001, Nippon Export and Investment Insurance (NEXI) was established as a subsidiary to METI to support global business expansion assets, and in 2017, this became a stand-alone company owned by the government. Similar to the private sector where the DX requires a strategic pivot and employee reskilling, the government is also undergoing a qualitative change in addition to reorganization and power alignment.

7 Conclusion: The DX and Japan's New Political Economy

The purpose of this Element is to explain the economic and social shifts currently underway in Japan, and to lay out how Japan's political economy has begun to change to take advantage of the hand that Japan has been dealt.

The simultaneous arrival of demographic change and the DX are a certainty for Japan. Neither can be stopped. Together, they are triggering three tectonic shifts that also affect the country's political economy and government–business relations. First, the DX is borderless and unleashes a global race. It is inescapable, and it cannot be won through domestic policies alone. Toyota, like many other companies, has research offices, venture investments, and research alliances in Silicon Valley, Israel, Singapore, and many places in between. Domestic politics and policymaking need to be recalibrated to address the impact of global competition.

Second, the DX ushers in the next level of VUCA, a term that became a catchphrase in Japan in the 2010s. Unlike in the postwar years when the developmental goal was clear, it is highly uncertain which technologies are going to attract the most use cases in the future. In this uncertain setting, each company competes on its own, with differentiated deep technology bets in unchartered territories. These technologies straddle former sectoral boundaries of economic activity, rendering industry-based policies useless and forcing a shift to industry structure-based policymaking.

Third, the DX requires employee specialization and reskilling, just at a time when Japan's workforce is beginning to shrink. This brings two opportunities: legacy sectors that face succession issues can be phased out with much less societal stress, and human resource management practices can be adjusted in ways to help society and employees embrace the new technologies more easily than may be the case elsewhere.

Thus, Japan's twin dilemmas – the ageing and shrinking society and the digital disruption – offer an opportunity to exploit the "lucky moment." Advances in AI/machine learning, big data, 5G constant connectivity, and autonomous systems and robotics help compensate for the shrinking workforce, just as the ageing society with its new needs may open the doors to "society 5.0," a different lifestyle design enabled by new technologies to improve connectivity and "as-a-service" offerings.

The trends we have described present tremendous opportunities for Japanese firms and some, particularly the larger and more internationalized ones, have already begun taking advantage of them. Of course, diffusing those gains across the entire economy will represent significant challenges even for Japan's revised and strengthened political and business leaders. We will only know over time how Japan's new political economy can address the threats and challenges caused by fast technological change, including inequality, diversity, and the educational and rural–urban divides.

How can we gauge whether Japan is successful in deploying the DX to solving the societal and business challenges that it is currently facing? One challenge is that our current approaches to interpreting data from Japan are also disrupted by the DX. Standard metrics such as employment by sector, or sectoral contribution to GDP, or even GDP itself no longer fully capture the reality of economic activity in Japan, or Japan's ranking in global economic contribution. Even productivity measures are not directly comparable, given Japan's very different social welfare and aging society profiles. Meanwhile, business models are shifting, and revenues are increasingly generated globally. Industrial policy is turning into industry structure policy, away from pushing specific "winning industries" and toward focusing on cross-sectoral issues, from environmental upgrades to preparing all firms for the DX. To assess these developments, we will need to look at new data in new ways.

Realizing these disruptions, the government has begun to reorganize and redesign policy objectives. The creation of the Digital Agency represents a rethinking of how ministries should be organized around themes and tasks instead of industries, and how policies are shifting from domestic coordination to enabling global competitiveness.

For companies, the DX and "industry 4.0" demand adjustments to the design and operations of business, not just in terms of business models and income generation but also hiring and employment. The DX greatly reduces time and location specificity, diminishes the benefits of mass production, and challenges the underlying logic of value creation and value capture. The "2025 IT cliff," often seen as a calamity, represents yet another opportunity to launch a complete architecture change, including novel business strategies, work processes, and operations logics.

Employees will no longer be cogs, as companies shift to hiring talent for special assignments that require advanced expertise. "Society 5.0" brings a new purpose, and new trade-offs between rights and responsibilities – between employers and employees, within families, and across society. Reskilling may be daunting to many, but it also presents opportunities for renewal and advancement that can be motivating and invigorating. Efficiency and productivity will be valued more, and many of the DX technology offerings will be seen as welcome solutions to those ends.

The state does not really have a choice but to adjust. The DX and demographic change will happen regardless of what the state does. It can encourage and allow companies to place riskier bets. It can enable DX advances through education reforms and workstyle revisions, as it has already begun. The task for the state is to define a new role for itself so that it can help Japan embrace and exploit this fortuitous DX moment.

This means that a new quid pro quo is emerging in Japan's political economy. No longer does the state help companies grow, while companies provide welfare and employees concede to corporate strategies. A new system of rights and responsibilities is to be forged, with trade-offs likely to be characterized by more diversity and individuality, within industries and companies as well as employees. The state will likely find its role as enabling companies to compete, while designing new ways of compensating those that cannot. This will require the collection of more tax revenues, which companies can presumably pay if their burden in providing corporate welfare is reduced. The top talent can now shape their own careers based on specialization and job attractiveness. Lifetime employment may go away for some, but long-term work relations are likely to remain for the remainder of the workforce, because the labor shortage increases the competition for workers across all industries. The DX will critically shape this newly emerging social contract, as it affects corporate strategies, individual career design, and the state's options.

In the VUCA world, there are many things that can wrong, including betting on the wrong technologies or leaving too many parts of society behind. But the important takeaway is that Japan is a step ahead and has already fully embraced change. It would be a mistake to use old metrics of success to assess the emerging industrial architecture, and it would be equally misleading to consider Japan as trailing. Japan is not behind. In fact, its reshaping of the social contract, its forward-looking firms, and the commitment to a sustainable transition in face of dual disruptions make it the frontrunner.

Japan's experience with the DX and demographic change will also shape how other countries assess the new risks and opportunities of the future. South Korea and China are now facing similar dynamics of demographic change combined with technology opportunities. It would be speculative at this time to say what we can learn from their experiences. But watching Japan and other places in Asia will offer important insights going forward.

References

Abegglen, James C., and George Jr. Stalk. 1985. *Kaisha – The Japanese Corporation: How Marketing, Money, and Manpower Strategy, Not Management Style, Make the Japanese World Pace-Setters*. New York: Basic Books.

Acemoglu, Daron, and Pascual Restrepo. 2020. "Robots and Jobs: Evidence from US Labor Markets." *Journal of Political Economy* 128(6): 2188–244.

Amyx, Jennifer. 2004. *Japan's Financial Crisis: Institutional Rigidity and Reluctant Change*. Princeton: Princeton University Press.

Amyx, Jennifer, and Peter Drysdale (eds.). 2003. *Japanese Governance: Beyond Japan Inc*. London: Taylor & Francis Group.

Anchordoguy, Marie. 1989. *Computers, Inc. – Japan's Challenge to IBM*. Cambridge, MA: Harvard University Press.

Aoki, Masahiko, and Hugh Patrick (eds.). 1994. *The Japanese Main Bank System: Its Relevance for Developing and Transforming Economies*. New York: Oxford University Press.

BCG (Boston Consulting Group/Hello Tomorrow). 2019. *The Dawn of the Deep Tech Ecosystem*. https://media-publications.bcg.com/BCG-The-Dawn-of-the-Deep-Tech-Ecosystem-Mar-2019.pdf

Brynjolfsson, Erik, and Andrew McAfee. 2016. *The Second Machine Age: Work, Progress, and Prosperity in a Time of Brilliant Technologies*. New York: W. W. Norton.

Buche, Ivy, Howard Yu, and Thomas Malnight. 2016. "Recruit Japan: Harnessing Data to Create Value." Case Study IMD824.

Cabinet Office. 2019. *AI Senryaku 2019* (AI Strategy 2019). www.maff.go.jp/j/kanbo/tizai/brand/attach/pdf/ai-15.pdf

Cabinet Office. 2020a. *Reiwa 2nenpan kōreika shakai hakusho* (2020 White Paper on the Ageing Society). www8.cao.go.jp/kourei/whitepaper/w-2020/gaiyou/02pdf_indexg.html

Cabinet Office. 2020b. *Ministerial Meeting on Digital Transformation*, September 23 2020" https://japan.kantei.go.jp/99_suga/actions/202009/_00004.html

Calder, Kent E. 1988. *Crisis and Compensation: Public Policy and Political Stability in Japan, 1949–1986*. Princeton: Princeton University Press.

Calder, Kent E. 1989. "Elites in an Equalizing Role: Ex-Bureaucrats as Coordinators and Intermediaries in the Japanese Government-Business Relationship." *Comparative Politics* 21(4): 379–403.

Cole, Robert E., and Yoshifumi Nakata. 2014. "The Japanese Software Industry: What Went Wrong and What Can We Learn from it?" *California Management Review* 57(1): 16–43.

Curtis, Gerald L. 1988. *The Japanese Way of Politics*. New York: Columbia University Press.

Curtis, Gerald L. 1999. *The Logic of Japanese Politics*. New York: Columbia University Press.

Deloitte Tohmatsu Consulting (ed.). 2020. *Hatarakikata kaikaku no jittai chōsa 2020 no kekka o happyō* (Results of Survey on the Implementation of Workstyle Reform 2020). www2.deloitte.com/jp/ja/pages/about-deloitte/art icles/news-releases/nr20200205.html

Dore, Ronald. 1973. *British Factory – Japanese Factory: The Origins of National Diversity in Industrial Relations*. Berkeley: University of California Press.

Dore, Ronald. 1986. *Flexible Rigidities: Industrial Policy and Structural Adjustment in the Japanese Economy, 1970–1980*. London: The Athlone Press.

Dore, Ronald. 1987. *Taking Japan Seriously: A Confucian Perspective on Leading Economic Issues*. Stanford: Stanford University Press.

Estevez-Abe, Margarita. 2008. *Welfare and Capitalism in Postwar Japan: Party, Bureaucracy, and Business*. Cambridge: Cambridge University Press.

Ford, Martin. 2016. *Rise of the Robots: Technology and the Threat of a Jobless Future*. New York: Basic Books.

Glosserman, Brad. 2019. *Peak Japan: The End of Great Ambitions*. Washington, DC: Georgetown University Press.

Haggard, Stephan. 2018. *Developmental States*. Cambridge: Cambridge University Press.

Himino, Ryozo. 2021. *The Japanese Banking Crisis*. London: Palgrave-McMillan.

Holst, Hajo, Katsuki Aoki, Gary Herrigel et al. 2020. "Gemba-Digitalisierung." *Zeitschrift für wirtschaftlichen Fabrikbetrieb* 115(9): 629–33.

Hoshi, Takeo, and Anil Kashyap. 2001. *Corporate Financing and Corporate Governance in Japan: The Road to the Future*. Boston: MIT Press.

Hoshi, Takeo, and Phillip Y. Lipscy (eds.). 2021. *The Political Economy of the Abe Government and Abenomics Reforms*. Cambridge: Cambridge University Press.

IPA (Jōhō shori suishin kikō) (ed.). 2020. *IT Jinzai Hakusho 2020: Ima koso DX o kasoku seyo* (White Paper on HR Practices for the IT Sector: The DX is Now Accelerating). www.ipa.go.jp/files/000085255.pdf

Ito, Takatoshi, and Takeo Hoshi. 2021. *The Japanese Economy* (2nd ed.). Cambridge, MA: MIT Press.

JFTC (Japan Fair Trade Commission). 2020. *Jigyōshadantai no katsudō ni kan suru dokusen kinshi-hō no shishin* (Guideline on Antitrust Law Rules Regarding the Activities of Trade Associations). www.jftc.go.jp/dk/guide line/unyoukijun/jigyoshadantai_files/jigyoshadantaigl.pdf

JIL (Japan Institute for Labor Policy and Training). 2018. "Work Style Reform Bill Enacted." *Japan Labor Issues* 2(10): 2–7.

Johnson, Chalmers. 1974. "The Reemployment of Retired Government Bureaucrats in Japanese Big Business." *Asian Survey* 14: 953–65.

Johnson, Chalmers. 1982. *MITI and the Japanese Miracle – The Growth of Industrial Policy, 1925–1975*. Stanford: Stanford University Press.

Johnson, Chalmers. 1999. "The Developmental State: Odyssey of a Concept." Pp. 32–60 in *The Developmental State*, edited by Meredith Woo-Cummings. Ithaca: Cornell University Press.

Katada, Saori. 2020. *Japan's New Regional Reality: Geoeconomic Strategy in the Asia-Pacific*. New York: Columbia University Press.

Kimura, Naonari, and Shunsuke Numata. 2018. *Mieruka 4.0: AI x IOT de "kase-guryoku" o torimodose!* (Visualing 4.0: How to Regain Profit-Earning Powers through AI x IOT). Tokyo: Nihon keizai shinbun shuppansha.

Kohno, Masaru. 2002. "A Changing Ministry of International Trade and Industry." Pp. 96–112 in *Japan Governance, Beyond Japan Inc.*, edited by Jennifer Amyx and Peter Drysdale. London: Routledge.

Komiya, Ryutarō, Masahiro Ōkuno, and Kotarō Suzumura (eds.). 1988. *Industrial Policy of Japan*. Tokyo: Academic Press.

Kōmuin sōken (ed.). 2021. *Kōmuin no shibōsha sannen renzoku genshō* (Number of Applicants for Public Service Positions Declines for the Third Consecutive Year). https://koumu.in/articles/1557f

Koo, Richard. 2011. "The World in Balance Sheet Recession: Causes, Cure, and Politics." *Real-World Economic Review* 58. www.paecon.net/PAEReview/issue58/Koo58.pdf

Krauss, Ellis S., and Robert J. Pekkanen. 2011. *The Rise and Fall of Japan's LDP: Political Party Organizations as Historical Institutions*. Ithaca: Cornell University Press.

Larke, Roy. 1994. *Japanese Retailing*. London: Routledge.

Lebo, Franklin Barr. 2018. *Between Democracy and Technocracy: Regulating Administrative Guidance in Japan*. London: Lexington Books.

Lincoln, James R., and Michael L. Gerlach. 2004. *Japan's Network Economy: Structure, Persistence, and Change*. Cambridge: Cambridge University Press.

Maclachlan, Patricia, and Kay Shimizu. 2021. "Japanese Agricultural Reform under Abenomics." Pp. 421–44 in *The Political Economy of the Abe Government and Abenomics Reforms*, edited by Takeo Hoshi and Phillip Y. Lipscy, Cambridge: Cambridge University Press.

Maclachlan, Patricia, and Kay Shimizu. 2022. *Betting on the Farm: Institutional Reform in Japanese Agriculture*. Ithaca: Cornell University Press.

McKinsey & Company, and ACCJ. 2021. *Japan Digital Agenda 2030: Big Moves to Restore Digital Competitiveness and Productivity*, Tokyo, February 2021, www.accj.or.jp/japan-digital-agenda-2030.

METI (Ministry of Economy, Trade and Industry). 2017. *Shin sangyō kōzō bijion: Hitori-hitorino, sekai no kadai o kaiketsu suru Nihon no shōrai* (New Industry Structure Vision: A Future for Japan that can Help Solve Global Problems). www.meti.go.jp/shingikai/sankoshin/shinsangyo_kozo/pdf/017_05_00.pdf

METI (Ministry of Economy, Trade and Industry). 2018a. *DX repōto: IT shisutemu "2025 nen no gake" no kokufuku to DX no honkakuteki na hatten* (Report on Digital Transformation: Overcoming of "2025 Digital Cliff" Involving IT Systems and Full-fledged Development of Efforts for Digital Transformation). www.meti.go.jp/shingikai/mono_info_service/digital_transformation/pdf/20180907_03.pdf

METI (Ministry of Economy, Trade and Industry). 2018b. *Arata na jidai no sangyō gijutsu seisaku ni tsuite* (Industrial Technology Policy for a new Era). www.meti.go.jp/shingikai/sankoshin/sangyo_gijutsu/kenkyu_innovation/pdf/007_02_00.pdf

METI (Ministry of Economy, Trade and Industry). 2018c. *Seizōgyō o meguru genjō to seisaku kadai: "Connected Industries" no shinka* (The Current Status of Manufacturing and Policy Tasks: The Progress of Connected Industries). www.meti.go.jp/shingikai/mono_info_service/air_mobility/pdf/001_s01_00.pdf

METI (Ministry of Economy, Trade and Industry). 2019a. *Dai yon-kai sangyō kaikaku ni muketa sangyō kōzō no genjō to kadai ni tsuite* (Report on the Current Situation and Future Tasks for the Industry Structure in the 4th Industrial Revolution). www.meti.go.jp/shingikai/sankoshin/2050_keizai/pdf/005_02_00.pdf

METI (Ministry of Economy, Trade and Industry). 2019b. *Rōdō shijō no kōzō henka no genjō to kadai ni tsuite* (On the Current Situation and Future Tasks of Structural Change in the Labor Market). www.meti.go.jp/shingikai/sankoshin/2050_keizai/pdf/005_03_00.pdf

METI (Ministry of Economy, Trade and Industry). 2020a. *Reiwa 3 nendo keizai-sangyōseisaku no jūten* (Main Points of Economic and Industrial

Policy for 2021), 27th Industry Structure Deliberation Council, September. www.meti.go.jp/shingikai/sankoshin/sokai/pdf/027_02_00.pdf

METI (Ministry of Economy, Trade and Industry). 2020b. *DX Repōto 2 [Chūkan torimatome]* (DX Report 2 [Interim Version]). www.meti.go.jp /press/2020/12/20201228004/20201228004-2.pdf

METI (Ministry of Economy, Trade and Industry). 2020c. *Jizokuteki na kigyō kachi no dōjō to jinteki-shihon ni kan suru kenkyūkai hōkokusho* (Report by the Study Group on Long-term Corporate Value Creation and Human Capital). www.meti.go.jp/shingikai/economy/kigyo_kachi_kojo/pdf/ 20200930_1.pdf

MEXT (Ministry of Education, Culture, Sports, Science and Technology). 2020. *Atarashii jidai no kōkō gakkō kyōiku no arikata waakingu gurūpu* (Summary of Working Group on High School Education in the New Era). www.mext.go.jp/content/20201111-mxt_koukou02-000011002_02.pdf

Miura, Mari. 2012. *Welfare through Work: Conservative Ideas, Partisan Dynamics and Social Protection in Japan.* Ithaca: Cornell University Press.

Mori, Isao. 2019. *Kantei Kanryō* (Cabinet Office Bureaucrats). Tokyo: Tankobon.

MRI (Mitsubishi Research Institute) (ed.). 2021. *3X – Kakushinteki na tekunor-ojii to komyuniti ga motarasu mirai* (The Three X: The Effects of Disruptive Technologies on Community). Tokyo: Diamond.

Muramatsu, Michio. 1981. *Sengo nihon no kanryōsei* (Japan's Postwar Bureaucracy). Tokyo: Toyo Keizai.

Muramatsu, Michio, and Ellis S. Krauss. 1984. "Bureaucrats and Politicians in Policymaking: The Case of Japan." *The American Political Science Review* 78(1): 126–46.

Muramatsu, Michio, and Ellis S. Krauss. 1987. "The Conservative Policy Line and the Development of Patterned Pluralism." Pp. 516–55 in *The Political Economy of Japan*, edited by Kozo Yamamura and Yasukichi Yasuba. Stanford: Stanford University Press.

Nakano, Koichi. 1998. "The Politics of Administrative Reform in Japan, 1993–1998: Toward a More Accountable Government?" *Asian Survey* 38(3): 291–309.

Namba, Tomoko. 2013. *Bukakkō keiei* (Leading a Bumpy Journey). Tokyo: Nikkei BP.

NEDO (New Energy Development Organization). 2018. *Heisei 29 nendo Nihon kigyō no mono to sābisu sofutobea no kokusai kyōsō pojishion ni kan suru jōhō shūshū* (Information Collection Regarding the Global Competitive Position of Japanese Manufacturing and Software Firms in 2017). Tokyo: NEDO/METI.

Nishiyama, Keita. 2021. *DX no shikōhō: Nihon keizai fukkatsu e no saikyō senryaku* (New DX Thinking: The Ultimate Strategy for Revising the Japanese Economy). Tokyo: Bungei Shunju.

OECD. 2021. *Creating Responsive Adult Learning Opportunities in Japan.* www.oecd.org/publications/creating-responsive-adult-learning-opportun ities-in-japan-cfe1ccd2-en.htm

Ozawa, Ichiro. 1994. *Blueprint for a New Japan: The Rethinking of a Nation.* Tokyo: Kodansha.

Patrick, Hugh, and Henry Rosovsky (eds.). 1976. *Asia's New Giant: How the Japanese Economy Works.* Washington, DC: Brookings Institution.

Patrick, Hugh T., and Thomas P. Rohlen. 1987. "Small-Scale Family Enterprises." Pp. 331–84 in *The Political Economy of Japan, Part 1: The Domestic Transformation,* edited by Kozo Yamamura and Yasukichi Yasuba. Stanford: Stanford University Press.

Pempel, T. J. 1974. "The Bureaucratization of Policymaking in Japan." *American Journal of Political Science* 18(40): 647–64.

Pempel, T. J. 1998. *Regime Shift: Comparative Dynamics of the Japanese Political Economy.* Ithaca: Cornell University Press.

Pfeffer, Jeffrey, and James N. Baron. 1988. "Taking the Workers Back Out: Recent Trends in the Structuring of Employment." *Research in Organizational Behavior* 10: 257–303.

Porter, Michael E., Hirotaka Takeuchi, and Mariko Sakakibara. 2000. *Can Japan Compete?* London: Macmillan Press.

Prahalad, C. K., and Gary Hamel. 1990. "The Core Competence of the Corporation." *Harvard Business Review* 68(3): 79–91.

Reed, Steven R., Kenneth Mori McElwain, and Kay Shimizu. 2009. *Political Change in Japan: Electoral Behavior, Party Realignment, and the Koizumi Reforms.* Stanford: Shorenstein Asia-Pacific Research Center.

RIETI (Research Institute of the Economy, Trade and Industry), Committee on the History of Japan's Trade and Industry Policy (ed.). 2020. *Dynamics of Japan's Trade and Industrial Policy in the Post Rapid Growth Era (1980–2000).* https://link.springer.com/book/10.1007/978-981-15-1987-1

Sato, Seizaburo, and Tetsuhisa Matsuzaki. 1986. *Jiminto Seiken (LDP Rule).* Tokyo: Chuo Koronsha.

Schaede, Ulrike. 1995. "The 'Old Boy' Network and Government-Business Relationships." *The Journal of Japanese Studies* 21(2): 293–317.

Schaede, Ulrike. 2000. *Cooperative Capitalism: Self-Regulation, Trade Associations, and the Antimonopoly Law in Japan.* Oxford: Oxford University Press.

Schaede, Ulrike. 2004. "Cooperating to Compete: Determinants of a Sanctuary Strategy among Japanese Firms." *Asian Business and Management* 3: 435–57.

Schaede, Ulrike. 2008. *Choose and Focus: Japanese Business Strategies for the 21st Century*. Ithaca: Cornell University Press.

Schaede, Ulrike. 2020. *The Business Reinvention of Japan: How to Make Sense of the New Japan, and Why It Matters*. Stanford: Stanford University Press.

Schaede, Ulrike. 2021. "Sōgōshoku no fukugyō/kengyō ga, Nihon ni innobeeshion o umidasu." *Nikkei Business Online KAISHA no saikō #7*. https://business.nikkei.com/atcl/gen/19/00235/052100007/

Schwartzman, David. 1993. *The Japanese Television Cartel: A Study Based on Matsushita v. Zenith*. Ann Arbor: University of Michigan Press.

Shirakawa, Masaaki. 2021. *Tumultuous Times: Central Banking in an Era of Crisis*. New Haven: Yale University Press.

SMEA (Small and Medium Enterprise Agency). 2019. *2019 nenban Chūshōkigyō hakusho: Reiwa jidai no chūshōkigyō no katsudō ni mukete* (2019 Small and Medium Enterprise White Paper: Toward Revising SME in the Reiwa Era), www.chusho.meti.go.jp/pamflet/hakusyo/2019/PDF/chusho/00Hakusyo_zentai.pdf

Solís, Mireya. 2017. *Dilemmas of a Trading Nation: Japan and the United States in the Evolving Asia-Pacific Order*. Washington, DC: Brookings Institution Press.

Solís, Mireya. 2020. "The Underappreciated Power: Japan after Abe." *Foreign Affairs* 99(6): 123–132.

Suzuki, Kenji. 2006. "The Changing Pattern of Amakudari Appointments, 1991–2000." Pp. 202–20 in *Institutional Change in Japan*, edited by Magnus Blomström and Sumner La Croix. London/New York: Routledge.

Takenaka, Harutaka. 2021. "Expansion of the Prime Minister's Power and Transformation of Japanese Politics." Pp. 43–67 in *The Political Economy of the Abe Government and Abenomics Reforms*, edited by Takeo Hoshi and Phillip Y. Lipscy. Cambridge: Cambridge University Press.

Tanaka, Yō. 2012. *Sebun-irebun owarinaki kakushin* (The Never-Ending Transformation of Seven-Eleven). Tokyo: Nikkei Bijinesu-jin bunko.

Toya, Tetsuro, and Jennifer A. Amyx. 2006. *The Political Economy of the Japanese Financial Big Bang: Institutional Change in Finance and Public Policymaking*. Oxford: Oxford University Press.

Toyama, Kazuhiko. 2020. *Kōporeeto toransufōmeeshion: Nihon no kaisha o tsukurikaeru* (Corporate Transformation: CX for DX). Tokyo: Bungei Shunju.

Vogel, Ezra F. 1979. *Japan as Number One: Lessons for America*. New York: Harper & Row.

Vogel, Steven K. 2006. *Japan Remodeled: How Government and Industry are Reforming Japanese Capitalism*. Ithaca: Cornell University Press.

Vogel, Steven K. 2018. "Japan's Labor Regime in Transition: Rethinking Work for a Shrinking Nation." *Journal of Japanese Studies* 44(2): 257–92.

Waldenberger, Franz. 2013. "'Company Heroes' versus 'Superstars': Executive Pay in Japan in Comparative Perspective." *Contemporary Japan* 25(2): 189–213.

Womack, James P., Daniel T. Jones, and Daniel Roos. 1990. *The Machine that Changed the World: The Story of Lean Production – Toyota's Secret Weapon in the Global Car Wars that is Now Revolutionizing World Industry*. New York: Simon and Schuster.

Yamamura, Kozo, and Yasukichi Yasuba (eds.). 1987. *The Political Economy of Japan, Vol. 1: The Domestic Transformation*. Stanford: Stanford University Press.

Acknowledgements

The authors are grateful to Grayson Sakos and Masahiro Naka for excellent research assistance, and to many interview partners for their insights. This Element has benefitted from helpful feedback by Christina Ahmadjian, Rick Dyck, Brad Glosserman, Stephan Haggard, Patricia Maclachlan, Alberto Moel, Gregory Noble, Yuma Yamada, and students in the UC San Diego class "Innovation in Japan," as well as an anonymous reviewer and the editors of this Elements series.

Cambridge Elements $\equiv$

Politics and Society in East Asia

Erin Aeran Chung
The Johns Hopkins University

Erin Aeran Chung is the Charles D. Miller Associate Professor of East Asian Politics in the Department of Political Science at the Johns Hopkins University. She specializes in East Asian political economy, international migration, and comparative racial politics. She is the author of *Immigration and Citizenship in Japan* (Cambridge, 2010, 2014; Japanese translation, Akashi Shoten, 2012) and *Immigrant Incorporation in East Asian Democracies* (Cambridge, 2020). Her research has been supported by grants from the Academy of Korean Studies, the Japan Foundation, the Japan Foundation Center for Global Partnership, the Social Science Research Council, and the American Council of Learned Societies.

Mary Alice Haddad
Wesleyan University, Connecticut

Mary Alice Haddad is the John E. Andrus Professor of Government, East Asian Studies, and Environmental Studies at Wesleyan University. Her research focuses on democracy, civil society, and environmental politics in East Asia as well as city diplomacy around the globe. A Fulbright and Harvard Academy scholar, Haddad is author of *Effective Advocacy: Lessons from East Asia's Environmentalists* (MIT, 2021), *Building Democracy in Japan* (Cambridge, 2012), and *Politics and Volunteering in Japan* (Cambridge, 2007), and co-editor of *Greening East Asia* (University of Washington, 2021), and *NIMBY Is Beautiful* (Berghahn Books, 2015). She has published in journals such as *Comparative Political Studies, Democratization, Journal of Asian Studies*, and *Nonprofit and Voluntary Sector Quarterly*, with writing for the public appearing in the *Asahi Shimbun, the Hartford Courant*, and *the South China Morning Post.*

Benjamin L. Read
University of California, Santa Cruz

Benjamin L. Read is a professor of politics at the University of California, Santa Cruz. His research has focused on local politics in China and Taiwan, and he also writes about issues and techniques in field research. He is author of *Roots of the State: Neighborhood Organization and Social Networks in Beijing and Taipei* (Stanford, 2012), coauthor of *Field Research in Political Science: Practices and Principles* (Cambridge, 2015), and co-editor of *Local Organizations and Urban Governance in East and Southeast Asia: Straddling State and Society* (Routledge, 2009). His work has appeared in journals such as *Comparative Political Studies, Comparative Politics, the Journal of Conflict Resolution, the China Journal, the China Quarterly*, and *the Washington Quarterly*, as well as several edited books.

About the Series

The Cambridge Elements series on Politics and Society in East Asia offers original, multidisciplinary contributions on enduring and emerging issues in the dynamic region of East Asia by leading scholars in the field. Suitable for general readers and specialists alike, these short, peer-reviewed volumes examine common challenges and patterns within the region while identifying key differences between countries. The series consists of two types of contributions: 1) authoritative field surveys of established concepts and themes that offer roadmaps for further research; and 2) new research on emerging issues that challenge conventional understandings of East Asian politics and society. Whether focusing on an individual country or spanning the region, the contributions in this series connect regional trends with points of theoretical debate in the social sciences and will stimulate productive interchanges among students, researchers, and practitioners alike.

Cambridge Elements ☰

Politics and Society in East Asia

Elements in the Series

The East Asian Covid-19 Paradox
Yves Tiberghien

State, Society and Markets in North Korea
Andrew Yeo

The Digital Transformation and Japan's Political Economy
Ulrike Schaede, Kay Shimizu

A full series listing is available at: www.cambridge.org/EPEA

Lightning Source UK Ltd.
Milton Keynes UK
UKHW020645050722
405403UK00010B/948

9 781108 925709